Cambridge Elements ≡

Elements in the Philosophy of Physics
edited by
James Owen Weatherall
University of California, Irvine

STRUCTURE AND EQUIVALENCE

Neil Dewar
University of Cambridge

CAMBRIDGE
UNIVERSITY PRESS

University Printing House, Cambridge CB2 8BS, United Kingdom

One Liberty Plaza, 20th Floor, New York, NY 10006, USA

477 Williamstown Road, Port Melbourne, VIC 3207, Australia

314–321, 3rd Floor, Plot 3, Splendor Forum, Jasola District Centre,
New Delhi – 110025, India

103 Penang Road, #05–06/07, Visioncrest Commercial, Singapore 238467

Cambridge University Press is part of the University of Cambridge.

It furthers the University's mission by disseminating knowledge in the pursuit of
education, learning, and research at the highest international levels of excellence.

www.cambridge.org
Information on this title: www.cambridge.org/9781108823760
DOI: 10.1017/9781108914581

© Neil Dewar 2022

First published 2022

A catalogue record for this publication is available from the British Library.

ISBN 978-1-108-82376-0 Paperback
ISSN 2632-413X (online)
ISSN 2632-4121 (print)

Structure and Equivalence

Elements in the Philosophy of Physics

DOI: 10.1017/9781108914581
First published online: February 2022

Neil Dewar
University of Cambridge
Author for correspondence: Neil Dewar, nad42@cam.ac.uk

Abstract: This Element explores what it means for two theories in physics to be equivalent (or inequivalent) and what lessons can be drawn about their structure as a result. It does so through a twofold approach. On the one hand, it provides a synoptic overview of the logical tools that have been employed in recent philosophy of physics to explore these topics: definition, translation, Ramsey sentences, and category theory. On the other, it provides a detailed case study of how these ideas may be applied to understand the dynamical and spatiotemporal structure of Newtonian mechanics – in particular, in light of the symmetries of Newtonian theory. In so doing, it brings together a great deal of exciting recent work in the literature and is sure to be a valuable companion for all those interested in these topics.

Keywords: structure, equivalence, physics, logic, symmetries

ISBNs: 9781108823760 (PB), 9781108914581 (OC)
ISSNs: 2632-413X (online), 2632-4121 (print)

Contents

Die Mathematiker sind eine Art Franzosen: redet man zu ihnen, so übersetzen sie es in ihre Sprache, und dann ist es alsobald ganz etwas anders.

J. W. von Goethe, *Maximen und Reflexionen*

Introduction

A perennial topic in philosophy of science in general – and philosophy of physics in particular – is the notion of *theoretical equivalence*. Sometimes, so the idea goes, two theories can say the same thing, even if they are formulated in somewhat different ways. Some such equivalences seem to follow from more general facts about the equivalence of certain linguistic expressions: if we express a theory in French and in German, or if we write it down once using Garamond font and again using Computer Modern, then the results are surely equivalent. More physics-specific cases of equivalence might include, for example, the different forms a theory takes in different coordinate systems; the relationship between wave and matrix mechanics in quantum theory; or the possibility of formulating General Relativity using a Lorentzian metric of signature $(3, 1)$, compared to a metric of signature $(1, 3)$. Some paradigm cases of *non*-equivalence would include Newtonian mechanics in comparison to relativistic mechanics, or statistical mechanics versus thermodynamics (not to mention entirely different theories, such as condensed matter physics compared to atmospheric physics). Finally, there is a large landscape of putative or contested cases – which is, unsurprisingly, also where the greatest philosophical interest lies. Are Lagrangian and Hamiltonian formulations of classical physics equivalent?[1] Can a formulation of Newtonian gravitation using curved spacetime be equivalent to a formulation employing flat spacetime?[2]

A second important topic is that of the *structure* of physical theories. For example, perhaps the central animating idea in the philosophical discussion of symmetries in physics is the idea that symmetries reveal *surplus structure*;[3] structural realists, meanwhile, contend that we should be realist only about the structural content of our theories – either because the epistemic warrant of realism only extends to structure, or because all there is in the world is structure.[4] Specific debates in the foundations of physics often turn on questions about how to treat some particular piece of structure: inertial structure, for instance, or

---

[1] See North (2009), Curiel (2014), Barrett (2015a).
[2] See Glymour (1977), Weatherall (2016).
[3] Redhead (1975); see the essays in Brading and Castellani (2003).
[4] Worrall (1989), French and Ladyman (2010), Frigg and Votsis (2011).

the structure of a wavefunction in configuration space.[5] Nevertheless, despite (or perhaps, because of) its centrality, it is not always entirely clear how the relevant notion of 'structure' in these debates is to be made out.

This Element is an attempt to survey some of the ways in which connecting the concept of structure with that of equivalence can be helpful. The core idea is that often, a claim or debate about the one concept can be reformulated as a claim or a debate about the other, via the following principle: equivalence is a matter of positing the same structure, and structure is that which is invariant across equivalence. So, for example, if someone proposes a particular way of cashing out what is meant by the structure of a theory, then that will bring in its wake a criterion of equivalence: theories are equivalent if they agree on that structure. On the other hand, if someone proposes a particular criterion of equivalence between theories, then we can assess that criterion's plausibility by seeing what structure it preserves, and what structure it does not preserve. As mentioned previously, one place where these themes are particularly prominent is the philosophy of symmetry: indeed, the idea that symmetries reveal surplus structure can be otherwise stated as the thesis that symmetry-related models of a theory are physically equivalent.

This nexus of ideas has been the focus of a great deal of exciting recent work, both technically and conceptually. However, one challenge for those interested in getting to grips with this literature is that it can sometimes feel split between philosophy of physics and philosophy of logic – making it potentially challenging for new readers to see how these ideas fit together. Hence, one goal for this Element is to try and bridge the gap between these two domains.[6] To that end, the first four sections of the Element are concerned with philosophy of logic (albeit with an eye to applications in philosophy of science). Sections 1 and 2 outline certain (related) ideas regarding definition and translation. Section 3 assesses the idea of using Ramsey sentences as a means of explicating a theory's structure – in particular, and as per the above, by assessing the notion of equivalence that this proposal induces. Section 4 then looks at how category-theoretic tools can be used, especially as giving a criterion of equivalence (either independently of or in conjunction with criteria derived from definability theory).

With these tools in hand, we start looking at Newtonian mechanics, as a case study for how these ideas play out in physics. Section 5 introduces the theory,

---

[5] For debates over inertial structure, see Knox (2014), Weatherall (2017), Read and Teh (2018); for debates about the wavefunction in configuration space, see Ney and Albert (2013) and references therein.

[6] This assumes that that gap is worth bridging, of course. For a dissenting view on that question, see Curiel (n.d.).

and sketches an analogy between that theory and the first-order theories discussed in the previous sections – and hence between Section 2's notion of a translation and the notion of a transformation between formulations of Newtonian mechanics in different coordinate systems. This gives us a reasonably attractive way to think of a *symmetry transformation*, namely as a translation between a theory and itself: this idea is introduced and discussed in Section 6, which also sketches why one might take symmetry-related models to be physically equivalent. Section 7 then considers the implications of that stance for the structure of the theory. It outlines what dispensing with symmetry-variant structure would involve, and what this would mean for equivalence relations between different formulations of the theory (drawing on ideas from Sections 3 and 4).

Finally, in Section 8, we take a step back to ask the question: how much light do formal criteria of equivalence shed on the issue of whether two theories say the same thing? Although this question is too large to be adequately answered there, I try to say something to push back on the idea that formal criteria of equivalence tell us little to nothing about genuine or bona fide equivalence.

Inevitably, to my eye this Element is marked as much by what it does not cover as by what it does. As we will touch on at various points, an omission that I feel keenly is the neglect of much exciting recent work on defining not just new predicates, but also new *sorts*. (More mundanely, we also do not discuss how to define new functions; the extension of what is said here to that case is relatively more trivial, however.) Similarly, we only discuss one case study from physics, which leaves aside many of the cases mentioned previously: the relationship between geometrised and non-geometrised theories, for instance, or that between Hamiltonian and Lagrangian mechanics. Still, sacrifices would have had to be made no matter how the Element was organised: I hope the reader can forgive these ones, as the price of not making others.

1 Definitions

We begin with the idea of *defining* structures in terms of one another. The motivating idea for this section is that if one is committed to a certain structure in physics, then one is often also committed to any structures definable in terms of that structure: consider, for example, the way in which a commitment to the structure of a Lorentzian metric on spacetime is standardly taken to bring with a commitment to the Levi-Civita connection on that spacetime.

However, in order to treat this idea of definability with appropriate rigour, we work exclusively in the context of first-order logic. Familiarity with the basic notions of first-order model theory will be assumed.[7] The non-logical vocabulary will be referred to as a *signature*, paradigmatically denoted by Σ. We will limit our attention to signatures that only contain predicate symbols. Where appropriate, the arity of a predicate P in a signature will be indicated by a parenthesised superscript, so that $P^{(n)}$ indicates that the predicate P takes n arguments. Form (Σ) denotes the set of (open and closed) Σ-formulae.

To prevent confusion with the general notion of structure discussed in this Element, we will refer to first-order structures as *Tarski models*. The domain of a Tarski model A will be denoted by $|A|$. A Tarski model of signature Σ will be referred to as a Σ-model. We write $A \models \phi$ to indicate that the Σ-model A satisfies $\phi \in$ Form (Σ). Given $a_1, \ldots, a_n \in |A|$, if the open formula $\phi(x_1, \ldots, x_n)$ is satisfied in A when each x_i is assigned to a_i, then we write $A \models \phi[a_1, \ldots, a_n]$. The extension of a predicate P in the structure A will be denoted by P^A. Given signatures Σ and Σ^+, where $\Sigma \subset \Sigma^+$, the reduct of a Σ^+-structure A to Σ will be denoted by $A|_\Sigma$.

We will only appeal to the semantic consequence relation: given sets of Σ-formulae Φ and Ψ, $\Phi \models \Psi$ iff for every Σ-model A which satisfies every $\phi \in \Phi$, $A \models \psi$ for every $\psi \in \Psi$. (So long as we are in the first-order context, of course, this will coincide with syntactic consequence via your favourite proof system.) We will abbreviate $\Phi \models \{\psi\}$ by $\Phi \models \psi$, and $\{\phi\} \models \psi$ by $\phi \models \psi$. A Σ-theory T is a set of Σ-sentences, and a model of T is a Σ-model A such that for every $\phi \in T$, $A \models \phi$. The class of models of T will be denoted by $\mathrm{Mod}(T)$. Two theories T_1 and T_2 are *logically equivalent* if $\mathrm{Mod}(T_1) = \mathrm{Mod}(T_2)$; equivalently, if $T_1 \models T_2$ and $T_2 \models T_1$.

1.1 Models

As a starting point, consider the question of what it is for two first-order structures to be equivalent: in the sense, let us suppose, that if one person puts forward one of these structures as their representation of some phenomenon, and another person puts forward the other, we would not take them to be disagreeing with one another.[8]

One possible answer would be that the structures must be isomorphic, if they are to be equivalent with one another. However, a little reflection suggests that this is too strict. Suppose that one person proffers the strict linear order S with three elements, and the other puts forward the weak linear order W with three

---

[7]　For an introduction to these notions, see, for example, Hodges (1993), Button and Walsh (2018), and Halvorson (2019).

[8]　For more discussion of the notion of 'sameness of structure' in the context of definability theory, see Button and Walsh (2018), chapter 5.

Figure 1 The strict linear order with three elements S. (Created using the tikzcd-editor at `https://tikzcd.yichuanshen.de/`.)

Figure 2 The weak linear order with three elements W. (Created using the tikzcd-editor at `https://tikzcd.yichuanshen.de/`.)

elements: see Figures 1 and 2. Certainly, these two structures are not isomorphic. Yet it seems odd to take our two interlocutors to be disagreeing in any substantive sense: it seems more natural to say that they have merely made different choices about which relation to use in describing the structure, i.e. whether to use $<$ or $\leq$.[9]

We can make this idea precise by introducing the concept of *definability*. Intuitively, a certain collection of elements (or tuples) in a structure is definable just in case it consists of precisely those elements (or tuples) matching a certain description. More formally:

Definition 1.1 Let A be a Σ-structure. A set $X \subseteq |A|^n$ is *definable in* A if and only if there is some Σ-formula $\phi(x_1, \ldots, x_n)$ such that

$$\langle a_1, \ldots, a_n \rangle \in X \text{ iff } A \models \phi[a_1, \ldots, a_n] \tag{1.1}$$

We will say that a function in a structure A is definable just in case its graph is: that is, a function $h : |A|^n \to |A|$ is definable in A just in case the set

$$\{\langle a_1, \ldots, a_n, b \rangle \in |A|^{n+1} : h(a_1, \ldots, a_n) = b\} \tag{1.2}$$

is definable in A.

Intuitively, S and W have the same structure because each is definable in terms of the other: we make this precise by using the concept of *definitional equivalence*. To see how this works, consider a third three-element structure L, over which both the strict and weak linear orderings apply: see Figure 3. Clearly L is an expansion of both S and W.[10] But the extensions of all predicates in L

---

9 Strictly speaking, the use of isomorphism as a criterion is even stricter than this. Since isomorphic structures must employ the same signature, we would have to regard the three-element strict linear order as inequivalent when it is represented using a relation whose symbol is $<$, compared to when it is represented using a symbol $\prec$! However, the observation above applies even to the natural weakening of isomorphism to allow for different choices of symbology (what Lutz (2015) calls *H-isomorphism*).

10 Recall that a Σ^+-structure A is an *expansion* of a Σ-structure B iff $\Sigma \subset \Sigma^+$ and $B = A|_\Sigma$.

Figure 3 A common definitional extension L of S and W. (Created using the tikzcd-editor at https://tikzcd.yichuanshen.de/.)

are definable in S, or in W. We say, therefore, that L is a *common definitional expansion* of both S and W:

Definition 1.2 Let A be a Σ-model and let B be a Σ^+-model. B is a *definitional expansion* of A if B is an expansion of A and for every symbol $F \in \Sigma^+ \setminus \Sigma$, F^B is definable in A.

When two structures have a common definitional expansion, we say that they are definitionally equivalent.

Definition 1.3 Let A_1 be a Σ_1-model and let A_2 be a Σ_2-model. A_1 and A_2 are *definitionally equivalent* if they have a common definitional expansion A^+, in signature $\Sigma_1 \cup \Sigma_2$.

Thus S and W are definitionally equivalent, as witnessed by their common definitional expansion L. Note that despite the name, definitional equivalence is not an equivalence relation, as it is not transitive.

Example 1.4 In the signature $\{P^{(1)}\}$, let $|A_1| = |A_2| = \{*\}$ (i.e. a singleton set); and let $P^{A_1} = \{*\}$ whereas $P^{A_2} = \varnothing$. Meanwhile, for signature $\{Q^{(1)}\}$, let $|B| = \{*\}$, and let $Q^B = \{*\}$. Then A_1 and A_2 are both definitionally equivalent to B, but they are not definitionally equivalent to one another.

Finally, we make some brief remarks regarding the relationship between definability and *invariance*.[11] A set of elements (or tuples) in a Tarski model is invariant if it is 'fixed' by all automorphisms of that model, that is:

Definition 1.5 Let A be a Σ-structure. A set $X \subseteq |A|^n$ is *invariant* in A if, for any automorphism $h : A \to A$, and any $a_1, \ldots, a_n \in |A|$,

$$\langle a_1, \ldots, a_n \rangle \in X \Rightarrow \langle h(a_1), \ldots, h(a_n) \rangle \in X \tag{1.3}$$

---

[11] We will return to the significance of invariance in Section 7. For more on grades of invariance and indiscernibility, see Caulton and Butterfield (2012) and Button and Walsh (2018), chapter 15.

Thus, for example, the extension of any predicate in Σ is guaranteed to be invariant (by the definition of automorphism). More generally, it turns out that the extension of any formula whatsoever is invariant: that is,

Theorem 1.6 Let A be a Σ-structure. For any set $X \subseteq |A|^n$, if X is definable then X is invariant.

Proof By induction on the complexity of formulae; left as exercise.

This link between definability and invariance can be put to philosophical work. For example, Malament (1977) argues that the standard simultaneity relation is the unique simultaneity relation definable from the structure of Minkowski spacetime together with an inertial observer. To show that the standard simultaneity relation is definable, Malament observes that it is simply the relation of orthogonality relative to the inertial observer's worldline. To show that it is the *only* relation definable in these terms, Malament shows that any other simultaneity relation will not be preserved under all the isometries of Minkowski spacetime that preserve the observer's worldline. Hence, Malament relies crucially on the fact that definability is a sufficient condition for invariance.

However, the converse is not generally true: not all invariant sets are definable. For example, consider a (standard) model of the natural numbers, in the usual signature of arithmetic. This model is *rigid*, in that it possesses no nontrivial automorphisms. As a result, every subset in the domain is invariant. Since there are $\aleph_0$-many natural numbers, there are $2^{\aleph_0}$-many such subsets. But the signature is finite, and so there can be at most only $\aleph_0$-many formulae (since each formula is itself a finite construction); and hence only at most $\aleph_0$-many definable subsets. That said, although in general a model might contain sets that are both indefinable and invariant, there is a partial result:

Theorem 1.7 [Finite Svenonius Theorem] Let A be a *finite* Σ-structure. For any set $X \subseteq |A|^n$, if X is invariant then X is definable.

The proof is nontrivial (see Halvorson, 2019, Proposition 6.7.13). A corollary of Theorem 1.7 is that if A is finite and rigid, then every subset of $|A|$ (or of $|A|^n$, for any n) is definable.

1.2 Theories

If we want to extend the notion of definitional equivalence to theories, then it suggests that we should regard theories as equivalent if all the terms employed in one theory are definable in the other, and vice versa. To spell this idea out, we introduce the (formal) notion of an *explicit definition*.

Definition 1.8 (Explicit definition) Given a signature Σ and a predicate $P^{(n)} \notin \Sigma$, an *explicit definition of P in terms of* Σ is a formula in signature $\Sigma \cup \{P\}$ of the form

$$\forall x_1 \ldots \forall x_n (P x_1 \ldots x_n \leftrightarrow \tau_P(x_1, \ldots, x_n)) \tag{1.4}$$

where τ_P is a Σ-formula.

Definition 1.9 Where $\Sigma \subset \Sigma^+$ and $P \in \Sigma^+ \setminus \Sigma$, a Σ^+-theory *explicitly defines P in terms of* Σ if it entails some explicit definition of P in terms of Σ.

Given a Σ-theory T, recall that a Σ^+-theory T^+ (where $\Sigma \subseteq \Sigma^+$) is an *extension* of T if T^+ entails all of T's theorems: that is, if for any sentence ϕ such that $T \vDash \phi$, $T^+ \vDash \phi$. Intuitively, an extension of a theory is one which says everything the first theory says, and perhaps more besides. A *definitional* extension of a theory is one that only supplements the original theory by explicit definitions. More precisely:

Definition 1.10 (Definitional extension) Let T be a Σ-theory, and let T^+ be a Σ^+-theory where $\Sigma \subset \Sigma^+$. We say that T^+ is a *definitional extension* of T if T^+ is logically equivalent to a theory of the form

$$T \cup \{\delta_P\}_{P \in \Sigma^+ \setminus \Sigma} \tag{1.5}$$

where, for each $P \in \Sigma^+ \setminus \Sigma$, δ_P is an explicit definition of P in terms of Σ.

It's straightforward to show that a definitional extension T^+ of another theory T will be a *conservative* extension of T: that is, that for every Σ-sentence ϕ, if $T^+ \vDash \phi$ then $T \vDash \phi$ (in other words, T^+ has no 'new' Σ-consequences compared to T). So in this sense, definitional extensions – unlike extensions in general – do not say anything new. In fact, we can use this to provide an alternative characterisation of the notion of definitional extension: given a Σ-theory T and a Σ^+-theory T', T' is a definitional extension of T just in case T' is a conservative extension of T, and for every symbol $P \in \Sigma^+ \setminus \Sigma$, T' explicitly defines P.[12]

---

[12] The concept of definitional extension is closely related to Nagel's characterisation of reduction (Nagel, 1979, §11.II): if we suppose that Nagel's 'bridge laws' make it possible to explicitly

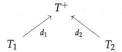

Figure 4 Definitional equivalence: d_1 and d_2 are definitional extensions of T_1 and T_2, respectively. (Created using the tikzcd-editor at https://tikzcd.yichuanshen.de/.)

Finally, just as two models are definitionally equivalent if they have a common definitional expansion, two theories are definitionally equivalent if they have a common definitional extension (see Fig. 4).

Definition 1.11 (Definitional equivalence of theories) Let T_1 be a Σ_1-theory, and let T_2 be a Σ_2-theory. T_1 and T_2 are *definitionally equivalent* if there is some theory T^+, in signature $\Sigma_1 \cup \Sigma_2$, which is a definitional extension of both T_1 and T_2.

Example 1.12 Consider the theory T_s of *strict partial orders*: this theory is in the signature $\{<^{(2)}\}$, and its axioms are

$$\forall x \neg(x < x) \tag{1.6}$$
$$\forall x \forall y (x < y \rightarrow \neg(y < x)) \tag{1.7}$$
$$\forall x \forall y \forall z (x < y \rightarrow (y < z \rightarrow x < z)) \tag{1.8}$$

On the other hand, consider the theory T_w of *weak partial orders*: this is in the signature $\{\leq^{(2)}\}$, and its axioms are

$$\forall x (x \leq x) \tag{1.9}$$
$$\forall x \forall y (x \leq y \rightarrow (y \leq x \rightarrow x = y)) \tag{1.10}$$
$$\forall x \forall y \forall z (x \leq y \rightarrow (y \leq z \rightarrow x \leq z)) \tag{1.11}$$

Here T_s and T_w are definitionally equivalent: if we supplement T_s with

$$\forall x \forall y (x \leq y \leftrightarrow (x < y \lor x = y)) \tag{1.12}$$

then we get a theory logically equivalent to the result of supplementing T_w with

$$\forall x \forall y (x < y \leftrightarrow (x \leq y \land x \neq y)) \tag{1.13}$$

and so T_s and T_w have a common definitional extension.

---

define the higher-level vocabulary in terms of the lower-level vocabulary, but that extending the lower-level theory by bridge laws is conservative, then we find that T_1 reduces to T_2 just in case some definitional extension of T_2 is also an extension of T_1. For more details, see Butterfield (2011a,b); Dewar (2019b).

As with definitional equivalence between models, definitional equivalence between theories is not transitive (and hence not an equivalence relation).

Example 1.13 Consider the theories

$$T_1 = \{\exists x \forall y (y = x), \forall x P x\} \tag{1.14}$$

$$T_2 = \{\exists x \forall y (y = x), \forall x \neg P x\} \tag{1.15}$$

$$T_3 = \{\exists x \forall y (y = x), \forall x Q x\} \tag{1.16}$$

where T_1 and T_2 are both in signature $\{P^{(1)}\}$, while T_3 is in signature $\{Q^{(1)}\}$. Then T_1 and T_2 are definitionally equivalent to T_3, but not definitionally equivalent to one another.

1.3 Theories and Models

Finally, we consider what kinds of relationships we can draw between syntactic and semantic notions of definability. In this context, a significant idea is that of *implicit definition*.[13]

Definition 1.14 (Implicit definition) Let Σ be a signature, and let $\Sigma^+ = \Sigma \cup \{P^{(n)}\}$. A Σ^+-theory T *implicitly defines P in terms of Σ* if for any two models A, B of T, if $A|_\Sigma = B|_\Sigma$ then $A = B$.

Intuitively, the idea of implicit definition is that the extensions of the Σ-predicates uniquely 'fix' the extension of P: provided that two models of T agree on the Σ-extensions, they have to agree on the extension of P. This idea is closely related to the notion of *supervenience*, as discussed in the metaphysics literature. In particular, McLaughlin and Bennett (2018) define 'strong global supervenience' as follows: '*A*-properties *strongly globally supervene* on *B*-properties iff for any worlds w_1 and w_2, every *B*-preserving isomorphism between w_1 and w_2 is an *A*-preserving isomorphism between them.' Adjusting to the model-theoretic context, we can formulate the following definition:

Definition 1.15 Let Σ be a signature, and let $\Sigma^+ = \Sigma \cup \{P\}$. *P strongly globally supervenes on Σ, relative to the Σ^+-theory T*, iff for any models A, B of T, any isomorphism $f : A|_\Sigma \to B|_\Sigma$ is an isomorphism from A to B (i.e. is such that f preserves the extension of P).

---

[13] This is not to be confused with the idea that a set of axioms, such as Hilbert's axioms for geometry, 'implicitly define' the meanings of the terms occurring therein.

So understood, strong global supervenience coincides with implicit definition.

Proposition 1.16 A symbol P is implicitly defined by T in terms of Σ iff it strongly globally supervenes on Σ relative to T.

Proof The right-to-left direction is immediate (since the identity map is always an isomorphism). For the other direction, suppose that P does not strongly globally supervene on Σ: so there exists a pair of models A, B of T and an isomorphism $f : \mathsf{A}|_\Sigma \to \mathsf{B}|_\Sigma$ that does not preserve P. We can then define a Σ^+ structure A' over the domain of A by the conditions that $\mathsf{A}'|_\Sigma = \mathsf{A}|_\Sigma$ and $P^{\mathsf{A}'} = f^{-1}[P^{\mathsf{B}}]$. Then A' will also be a model of T (since it is isomorphic to B); so we have a pair of models A, A' of T such that $\mathsf{A}'|_\Sigma = \mathsf{A}|_\Sigma$ yet $\mathsf{A}' \neq \mathsf{A}$ – and hence P is not implicitly defined by T in terms of Σ.

More remarkably, implicit definition turns out to coincide with explicit definition, at least in the context of first-order theories: this result is known as *Beth's theorem*.[14]

Theorem 1.17 (Beth's theorem) Let T be a Σ^+-theory, where $\Sigma^+ = \Sigma \cup \{R\}$. Then T explicitly defines R in terms of Σ iff T implicitly defines R in terms of Σ (and hence iff R supervenes on Σ relative to T).

The left-to-right direction of Beth's theorem is straightforward. However, the right-to-left direction is somewhat surprising: it is not at all obvious that the implicit definition of R encoded in the class of models of T can be parlayed into an explicit (and finite!) definition. The proof of this direction is correspondingly nontrivial (see Halvorson, 2019, §6.7). Indeed, Beth's theorem is a rather special feature of first-order logic. In higher-order logics (such as second-order logic, discussed in Section 3), Beth's theorem does not hold.

We can use Beth's theorem to relate definitional equivalence to a more 'semantic' characterisation of equivalence.[15] First, given signatures $\Sigma \subseteq \Sigma^+$, let us say that the *reduct map* is the map from the class of Σ^+-structures to the class of Σ-structures given by taking reducts (i.e. the map $\mathsf{A} \mapsto \mathsf{A}|_\Sigma$). So, a Σ^+-theory T implicitly defines $\Sigma^+ \setminus \Sigma$ in terms of Σ iff the reduct map is injective over $\mathrm{Mod}(T)$.

---

[14] As a result, in contexts where Beth's theorem holds, it is not so easy to have supervenience without reduction (if footnote 12's characterisation of reduction in terms of definitional extension is accepted). For more on this, see Hellman and Thompson (1975), List (2019), (Halvorson, 2019, §6.7), Dewar (2019b), and Dewar et al. (2019).

[15] The below follows de Bouvère (1965).

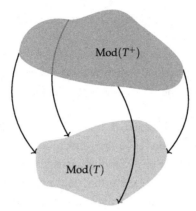

Figure 5 T^+ is a semantically conservative extension of T iff the reduct map
from $\text{Mod}(T^+)$ to $\text{Mod}(T)$ is surjective.

Note that a Σ^+-theory T^+ is an extension of a Σ-theory T iff the reduct map
is a map from $\text{Mod}(T^+)$ to $\text{Mod}(T)$: that is, T^+ is an extension of T iff given
any model M of T^+, M$|_\Sigma$ is a model of T.[16] If T^+ is an extension of T and the
reduct map is a *surjective* map from $\text{Mod}(T^+)$ to $\text{Mod}(T)$, then we will say that
T^+ is a *semantically conservative* extension of T (see Fig. 5): in other words,
T^+ is a semantically conservative extension of T iff for every model M of T,
there is some model M^+ of T^+ such that $M^+|_\Sigma = M$. Where disambiguation
is necessary, we will refer to the earlier notion of conservativity as *syntactic*
conservativity.[17] The two notions of conservation are related as follows:[18]

Proposition 1.18 If T^+ is a semantically conservative extension of T then it
is a syntactically conservative extension, but not vice versa.

Proof   See Lutz (2012), §6.11.2, or Button and Walsh (2018), §3.B.

All this suggests a semantic way of spelling out the ideas in this section.
Following de Bouvère (1965), we will describe the semantic analogue of a
definitional extension as a definitional *enrichment*, and the semantic analogue
of definitional equivalence as *coalescence*.

---

[16] For the proof, we need the fact that given any set of Σ-sentences Φ, then for any Σ^+-model A,
    A $\models \Phi$ iff A$|_\Sigma \models \Phi$. Given this, we can reason as follows: if there is some Σ-sentence ϕ such
    that $T \models \phi$ but $T^+ \not\models \phi$, then there is some model M of T^+ such that M $\not\models \phi$ and (hence)
    M$|_\Sigma \not\models \phi$; and so M$|_\Sigma \not\models T$. The other direction is similar.

[17] The terminology of 'syntactically' and 'semantically' conservative extensions is drawn from
    Lutz (2012), who in turn attributes it to Przełęcki (1969). Button and Walsh (2018) use the terms
    'consequence-conservative' and 'expansion-conservative' to describe the same distinction.

[18] At least in the first-order case: see Section 3 and Button and Walsh (2018), chapter 3.

Definition 1.19 Let T be a Σ-theory and let T^+ be an extension of T in the signature Σ^+. Then T^+ is a *definitional enrichment* of T if and only if T^+ is a semantically conservative extension of T, which implicitly defines $\Sigma^+ \setminus \Sigma$ in terms of Σ.

Put another way, T^+ is a definitional enrichment of T just in case the reduct map is a bijective map between $\mathrm{Mod}(T^+)$ and $\mathrm{Mod}(T)$.

Definition 1.20 Let T_1 and T_2 be Σ_1- and Σ_2-theories, respectively. Then T_1 and T_2 are *coalescent* iff there is a $(\Sigma_1 \cup \Sigma_2)$-theory T^+ which is a definitional enrichment of T_1 and of T_2.

However, in virtue of Beth's theorem, these notions turn out to be not just analogous to their syntactic cousins, but identical with them.

Theorem 1.21 A Σ^+-theory T^+ is a definitional extension of a Σ-theory T iff T^+ is a definitional enrichment of T.

Proof Suppose that T^+ is a definitional extension of T. Without loss of generality, we will suppose that T^+ takes the form $T \cup \{\delta_P\}_{P \in \Sigma^+ \setminus \Sigma}$, where for each predicate $P \in \Sigma^+ \setminus \Sigma$, δ_P takes the form (1.4). So by the trivial direction of Beth's theorem (Theorem 1.17), T^+ implicitly defines $\Sigma^+ \setminus \Sigma$ in terms of Σ. We therefore need only to show that T^+ is a semantically conservative extension of T. So let $\mathtt{M}$ be a model of T. Define $\mathtt{M}^+$ as an extension of $\mathtt{M}$ by the condition that for any symbol $P \in \Sigma^+ \setminus \Sigma$, $P^{\mathtt{M}^+} = \tau_P^{\mathtt{M}}$. Then, by construction, $\mathtt{M}^+ \models \delta_P$ for any $P \in \Sigma^+ \setminus \Sigma$, and so $\mathtt{M}^+ \models T^+$. So T^+ is a semantically conservative extension of T.

In the other direction, if T^+ is a definitional enrichment of T, then T^+ is a syntactically conservative extension of T (since semantic conservation entails syntactic conservation) and T^+ explicitly defines $\Sigma^+ \setminus \Sigma$ in terms of Σ (by the non-trivial direction of Beth's theorem). Hence, T^+ is a definitional extension of T.

Corollary 1.22 Let T_1 and T_2 be Σ_1- and Σ_2-theories, respectively. Then T_1 and T_2 are definitionally equivalent iff they are coalescent.[19]

The above is only a partial overview of the rich territory of definability theory, and is limited in some significant respects. For one thing, we have said nothing of the notion of definability with *parameters*, which plays a key role

---

[19] This is given as Theorem 2 in de Bouvère (1965).

in model theory.[20] Moreover, we have not engaged with the concept of *generalised* definitional extensions, also known as Morita extensions.[21] Intuitively, just as the definitions surveyed here permit one to define new predicates in terms of the hold, generalised definitions permit the definition of new *sorts*: as a result, the generalised definitional extension of a theory may, intuitively speaking, quantify over objects constructed out of the objects of the original theory. So generalised definitional equivalence gives a criterion of equivalence between theories that disagree not just over ideology but also over ontology.[22]

Nevertheless, we have been able to touch on some key ideas. First, we have seen that there is a close link between definability and invariance. Second, we have seen that we can apply the notions of definability to individual structures, or to theories (which correspond to classes of structures). Finally, and perhaps most importantly, we have seen that many ideas admit of an explication both in syntactic terms (i.e. in terms of theories and sentences) and semantic terms (i.e. in terms of models), and that spelling out the relationship between them can be illuminating.

2 Translation

In the previous section, we looked at how the concept of *definition* could be used to articulate criteria of equivalence between models and theories. This section considers a closely related notion, namely that of *translation*. We begin by considering the relation of 'codetermination', which we can think of as expressing a kind of intertranslatability condition on models; we then go on to consider how to translate between two theories, and how this is associated with certain relationships between the theories' classes of models.

2.1 Codetermination

Consider again the example of S and W in the previous section. There, we noted that these Tarski models could each be definitionally expanded to a common Tarksi model L. However, we can also observe that the extensions of each are definable in the other 'directly', in the following sense: the set $\leq^W$ is definable in S, by the two-place formula

$$x < y \lor x = y \tag{2.1}$$

---

[20] See (Hodges, 1993, chapter 2) or (Button and Walsh, 2018, §1.13).
[21] See Andréka et al. (2008), Barrett and Halvorson (2016b).
[22] See Quine (1951).

and the set $<^S$ is definable in W, by the two-place formula

$$x \leq y \wedge x \neq y \tag{2.2}$$

In light of this fact, we say that the Tarski models S and W are *codeterminate*.[23]

Definition 2.1 Given a Σ_1-model A_1 and a Σ_2-model A_2, the models A_1 and A_2 are *codeterminate* if and only if for every Σ_1-predicate F, F^{A_1} is definable in A_2, and for every Σ_2-predicate G, G^{A_2} is definable in A_1.

Note that like definitional equivalence, codetermination presupposes the sharing of a domain: if A_1 and A_2 are codeterminate, then $|A_1| = |A_2|$.

Definitional equivalence and codetermination are closely related, but not quite the same: in effect, definitional equivalence is codetermination plus agreement on shared vocabulary.

Proposition 2.2 Let A_1 and A_2 be Σ_1- and Σ_2-models, respectively. Then A_1 and A_2 are definitionally equivalent iff A_1 and A_2 are codeterminate, and $A_1|_{\Sigma_1 \cap \Sigma_2} = A_2|_{\Sigma_1 \cap \Sigma_2}$.

Proof First, definitional equivalence entails codetermination: if A^+ is a common definitional expansion of A_1 and A_2, then for any predicate $F \in \Sigma_1$, $F^{A_1} = F^{A^+}$, and hence is definable in A_2; the same goes for any predicate of Σ_2. Moreover, if $F \in \Sigma_1 \cap \Sigma_2$, then $F^{A^+} = F^{A_1} = F^{A_2}$; so $A_1|_{\Sigma_1 \cap \Sigma_2} = A_2|_{\Sigma_1 \cap \Sigma_2}$. This proves the left-to-right half of the proposition.

In the other direction, if A_1 and A_2 are codeterminate and $A_1|_{\Sigma_1 \cap \Sigma_2} = A_2|_{\Sigma_1 \cap \Sigma_2}$, then we can define a $(\Sigma_1 \cup \Sigma_2)$-model A^+ by the conditions

- $|A^+| = |A_1| = |A_2|$;
- for every $F \in \Sigma_1$, $F^{A^+} = F^{A_1}$; and
- for every $F \in \Sigma_2$, $F^{A^+} = F^{A_2}$.

The agreement on shared vocabulary ensures that the second and third conditions are compatible with one another. It follows that A^+ is a common definitional expansion of A_1 and A_2: for every $F \in \Sigma_1$, F^{A^+} is definable in A_2, and vice versa. Hence, A_1 and A_2 are definitionally equivalent.

Corollary 2.3 Let A_1 and A_2 be Σ_1- and Σ_2-models, respectively, where $\Sigma_1 \cap \Sigma_2 = \varnothing$ (i.e. over disjoint signatures). Then A_1 and A_2 are definitionally equivalent if and only if they are codeterminate.

---

[23] Winnie (1986), Barrett (2020).

Thus definitional equivalence entails codetermination, but not vice versa: for example, the Tarski models A_1 and A_2 from Example 1.4 are codeterminate to one another. It is easy to show that codetermination is an equivalence relation.

2.2 Translations between Theories

We have seen that one way in which theories can be related to one another is if the structures they each employ are interdefinable. We now turn to another kind of relationship between theories in which one might be interested: that of *intertranslatability*. We will find that these two notions – interdefinability and intertranslatability – are very closely connected.[24]

The basic idea of translating one theory into another is that we can systematically replace expressions of the first theory's language by expressions of the second theory's language, in such a way that all theorems of the first theory are converted into theorems of the second theory. More precisely,

Definition 2.4 Given signatures Σ_1 and Σ_2, a *dictionary* from Σ_1 to Σ_2 is a map τ associating each predicate $P^{(n)} \in \Sigma_1$ with an n-place Σ_2-formula τP.

Given a dictionary, we define a map $\tau :$ Form $(\Sigma_1) \rightarrow$ Form (Σ_2). Given any Σ_1-formula ϕ, the Σ_2-formula $\tau\phi$ is defined as follows (where we use $\equiv$ to indicate metalinguistic identity):

- If $\phi \equiv P x_1 \ldots x_n$, then $\tau\phi \equiv (\tau P)(x_1, \ldots, x_n)$.
- If $\phi \equiv \neg\psi$, then $\tau\phi \equiv \neg\tau\psi$.
- If $\phi \equiv (\psi_1 \rightarrow \psi_2)$, then $\tau\phi \equiv (\tau\psi_1 \rightarrow \tau\psi_2)$.
- If $\phi \equiv \forall x \psi$, then $\tau\phi \equiv \forall x (\tau\psi)$.

We are now in a position to define the notion of *translation* between theories: a translation is a map of this kind which preserves theoremhood.

Definition 2.5 (Translation) Let T_1 be a Σ_1-theory, and T_2 a Σ_2-theory, and let τ be a dictionary from Σ_1 to Σ_2. τ is a *translation* from T_1 to T_2 if for any Σ_1-sentence ϕ, if $T_1 \vDash \phi$ then $T_2 \vDash \tau\phi$.

How does the existence of a translation from one theory to another relate to the structures posited by the two theories? We can get some insight here by reflecting on how it is reflected in the relationships between the theories'

---

24 For more on translating between theories, see Button and Walsh (2018), chapter 5, or Halvorson (2019).

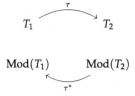

Figure 6 A translation τ and its dual map τ^*. (Created using the tikzcd-editor at https://tikzcd.yichuanshen.de/.)

classes of models. The key observation here is that a translation τ from one theory to another induces a 'dual map' τ^* from the models of the latter theory to those of the former (so the dual map goes 'in the other direction' from the translation – see Fig. 6).

Definition 2.6 (Dual map to a translation)   Let τ be a translation from the Σ_1-theory T_1 to the Σ_2-theory T_2. Given any Σ_2-model A, we define the Σ_1-model $\tau^*(A)$ as follows. First, the domain of $\tau^*(A)$ is the same as that of A, that is, $|\tau^*(A)| = |A|$. Second, for any $P^{(n)} \in \Sigma_1$, we define the extension of P in $\tau^*(A)$ as follows: for any $a_1, \ldots, a_n \in |A|$,

$$\langle a_1, \ldots, a_n \rangle \in P^{\tau^*(A)} \text{ iff } A \models (\tau P)[a_1, \ldots, a_n] \tag{2.3}$$

For any model A of T_2, $\tau^*(A)$ is a model of T_1 (see Proposition 2.8 below). So τ^* is a function from $\text{Mod}(T_2)$ to $\text{Mod}(T_1)$, which we refer to as the *dual map* to the translation τ.[25]

To prove the claim used in this definition – that if A is a model of T_2, then $\tau^*(A)$ is a model of T_1 – we need the following useful proposition.

Proposition 2.7   Let τ be a translation from the Σ_1-theory T_1 to the Σ_2-theory T_2. For any Σ_2-model A, and any Σ_1-sentence ϕ,

$$\tau^*(A) \models \phi \text{ iff } A \models \tau\phi \tag{2.4}$$

Proof   By induction on the complexity of formulae; left as exercise.

Given this proposition, the proof that the dual map to a translation preserves model-hood is straightforward.

---

[25] Here, we only discuss the case where we start with a translation, and obtain a corresponding dual map. However, one could also ask under what circumstances an arbitrary map $\text{Mod}(T_2) \rightarrow \text{Mod}(T_1)$ is the dual map to some translation $T_1 \rightarrow T_2$. Van Benthem and Pearce (1984) demonstrate that this is the case if and only if the map on models respects isomorphisms, ultraproducts, and domains.

Proposition 2.8 Let τ be a translation from the Σ_1-theory T_1 to the Σ_2-theory T_2. If A is a T_2-model, then $\tau^*(A)$ is a T_1-model.

Proof Suppose, for *reductio*, that A is a T_2-model but that $\tau^*(A)$ is not a T_1-model. Then there must be some sentence $\phi \in T_1$ such that $\tau^*(A) \not\models \phi$. Then, by Proposition 2.7, A $\not\models \tau\phi$. Since A is a T_2-model, it follows that $T_2 \not\models \tau\phi$. But by the definition of a translation, $T_2 \models \tau\phi$; so by contradiction, $\tau^*(A)$ must be a T_1-model.

What about the relationship between translation and definition? It turns out that there is a close relationship. First, we note a useful lemma.

Lemma 2.9 Let T be a Σ-theory, and let T^+ be a definitional extension of T to Σ^+ (where $\Sigma \subseteq \Sigma^+$). We know that for every $P \in \Sigma^+ \setminus \Sigma$ there is some Σ-formula τ_P such that

$$T^+ \models \forall x_1 \ldots \forall x_n (P x_1 \ldots x_n \leftrightarrow \tau_P(x_1, \ldots, x_n)) \tag{2.5}$$

We define a dictionary map $\tau : \Sigma^+ \to \Sigma$ by letting $\tau P \equiv \tau_P$ for any $P \in \Sigma^+ \setminus \Sigma$, and letting $\tau P \equiv P$ for any $P \in \Sigma$.

Then, for any Σ^+-formula $\phi(x_1, \ldots, x_n)$,

$$T^+ \models \forall x_1 \ldots \forall x_n (\phi \leftrightarrow \tau\phi) \tag{2.6}$$

Proof Induction on the complexity of ϕ (see Halvorson, 2019, Lemma 4.6.11).

We then have the following proposition.[26]

Proposition 2.10 Consider theories T_1 and T_2, in signatures Σ_1 and Σ_2, respectively. There exists a definitional extension T^+ of T_2 to $\Sigma_1 \cup \Sigma_2$ which is also an extension of T_1 if and only if there is a translation from T_1 to T_2 which acts as the identity on any shared vocabulary (i.e. on $\Sigma_1 \cap \Sigma_2$).

Proof For the left-to-right direction, suppose that T^+ is a definitional extension of T_2 and extension of T_1 to $\Sigma_1 \cup \Sigma_2$. We fix a dictionary $\tau^+ : \Sigma_1 \cup \Sigma_2 \to \Sigma_2$ as in Lemma 2.9. Let the dictionary $\tau : \Sigma_1 \to \Sigma_2$ be the restriction of τ^+ to Σ_1.

So now suppose that $T_1 \models \phi$, for some Σ_1-sentence ϕ. Since T^+ is an extension of T_1, we have that $T^+ \models \phi$; and hence by Lemma 2.9, $T^+ \models \tau\phi$.

---

[26] If we accept the definition of Nagelian reduction given in footnote 12 then this proposition has the following corollary: that T_1 Nagel-reduces to T_2 iff there is a translation from T_1 to T_2 which acts as the identity on $\Sigma_1 \cap \Sigma_2$.

Since $\tau\phi$ is a Σ_2-sentence, and since T^+ is a definitional (hence, conservative) extension of T_2, $T_2 \vDash \tau\phi$. Therefore, τ is a translation from T_1 to T_2; and by construction, τ acts as the identity on $\Sigma_1 \cap \Sigma_2$.

For the other direction, suppose that $\tau : T_1 \to T_2$ is a translation which acts as the identity on $\Sigma_1 \cap \Sigma_2$. Now consider the definitional extension T^+ of T_2 that is obtained by appending to T_2 explicit definitions of the following form for each predicate $P \in \Sigma_1 \setminus \Sigma_2$,

$$\forall x_1 \ldots \forall x_n (P x_1 \ldots x_n \leftrightarrow (\tau P)(x_1, \ldots, x_n)) \tag{2.7}$$

Furthermore, let the dictionary $\tau^+ : \Sigma_1 \cup \Sigma_2 \to \Sigma_2$ be the extension of τ obtained by setting $\tau^+ P \equiv P$ for all $P \in \Sigma_2$ (note that this is only possible because τ acts as the identity on $\Sigma_1 \cap \Sigma_2$).

Now suppose that $T_1 \vDash \phi$, for some Σ_1-sentence ϕ. Then $T_2 \vDash \tau\phi$, hence $T^+ \vDash \tau^+\phi$. So by Lemma 2.9, $T^+ \vDash \phi$. So T^+ is an extension of T_1, and the proposition follows.

2.3 Intertranslatability

Now, let us consider the question of how the notion of translation could be used to articulate a criterion of equivalence. The mere existence of a translation (as defined here) would be a very weak condition, and would have some very counter-intuitive consequences: it would mean, for example, that any theory would be equivalent to any strictly stronger theory (since inclusions are always translations) – indeed, that any theory is equivalent to some inconsistent theory! A more plausible criterion is to require the existence of a *pair* of translations. This criterion is known as *mutual translatability*.

Definition 2.11 Let T_1 and T_2 be theories of signatures Σ_1 and Σ_2, respectively. T_1 and T_2 are *mutually translatable* if there exist translations $\tau : T_1 \to T_2$ and $\sigma : T_2 \to T_1$.

However, mutual translatability is still a relatively weak notion, as the following example indicates.[27]

Example 2.12 Let $\Sigma_1 = \Sigma_2 = \{P^{(1)}\}$. Let

$$T_1 = \{\exists x \forall y (y = x)\} \tag{2.8}$$
$$T_2 = \{\exists x \forall y (y = x), \forall x P x\} \tag{2.9}$$

---

[27] This example is adapted from (Barrett and Halvorson, 2016a, Example 4).

Intuitively, one would not expect T_1 and T_2 to be equivalent: T_2 has only a single model up to isomorphism, and is therefore a *complete* theory, whereas T_1 is not complete.[28] Yet T_1 and T_2 are mutually translatable, via translations $\tau : T_1 \to T_2$ and $\sigma : T_2 \to T_1$ induced by the following dictionaries:

$$\tau : P \mapsto Px \tag{2.10}$$

$$\sigma : P \mapsto (Px \vee \neg Px) \tag{2.11}$$

In light of this, we introduce a yet stronger condition: not just that there exist a pair of translations, but that those translations be, in a certain sense, inverse to one another. The intuition here is that if we take some expression of our first theory's language, translate it into the second language, and then translate it back into the first language, we should – if the pair of translations really express an equivalence between the theories – get an expression with the same meaning as the expression with which we began. Formally, we cash out this condition of 'having the same meaning' as 'equivalent modulo the ambient theory'; the resulting criterion is known as *intertranslatability*.[29]

Definition 2.13 Let T_1 and T_2 be theories of signatures Σ_1 and Σ_2, respectively. T_1 and T_2 are *intertranslatable* if there exist translations $\tau : T_1 \to T_2$ and $\sigma : T_2 \to T_1$, such that for any Σ_1-formula $\phi(x_1, \ldots, x_n)$ and any Σ_2-formula $\psi(y_1, \ldots, y_m)$,

$$T_1 \vDash \forall x_1 \ldots \forall x_n (\phi \leftrightarrow \sigma\tau\phi) \tag{2.12a}$$

$$T_2 \vDash \forall y_1 \ldots \forall y_m (\psi \leftrightarrow \tau\sigma\psi) \tag{2.12b}$$

In such a case, we will say that τ and σ are *inverse translations* to one another.

As one might have expected from Propositions 2.2 and 2.10, intertranslatability and definitional equivalence turn out to be related in the following way.

Proposition 2.14 Consider theories T_1 and T_2, in signatures Σ_1 and Σ_2. Then T_1 is definitionally equivalent to T_2 if and only if T_1 and T_2 are intertranslatable relative to a pair of translations that act as the identity on $\Sigma_1 \cap \Sigma_2$.

Proof First, suppose that T_1 is definitionally equivalent to T_2: let T^+ be their common definitional extension. Define translations $\tau : T_1 \to T_2$ and

---

[28] Recall that a Σ-theory T is complete if for every Σ-sentence ϕ, either $T \vDash \phi$ or $T \vDash \neg\phi$.
[29] Barrett and Halvorson (2016a).

$\sigma : T_2 \rightarrow T_1$ as in the proof of Proposition 2.10; as there, note that these translations act as the identity on $\Sigma_1 \cap \Sigma_2$. Let $\phi(x_1, \ldots, x_n) \in$ Form (Σ_1). Then by a double application of Lemma 2.9, $T^+ \vDash \forall x_1 \ldots \forall x_n (\phi \leftrightarrow \sigma\tau\phi)$. But since $\sigma\tau\phi$ is a Σ_1-formula, and T^+ is a conservative extension of T_1, $T_1 \vDash \forall x_1 \ldots \forall x_n (\phi \leftrightarrow \sigma\tau\phi)$. The proof of (2.12b) is similar.

Second, suppose that T_1 and T_2 are intertranslatable, with $\tau : T_1 \rightarrow T_2$ and $\sigma : T_2 \rightarrow T_1$ being inverse translations that act as the identity on $\Sigma_1 \cap \Sigma_2$. Define a definitional extension T_2^+ of T_2 by appending to T_2 explicit definitions of the form (2.7) for each $P \in \Sigma_1$; define a definitional extension T_1^+ of T_1 in analogous fashion. Finally, let $\tau^+ : \Sigma_1 \cup \Sigma_2 \rightarrow \Sigma_2$ and $\sigma^+ : \Sigma_1 \cup \Sigma_2 \rightarrow \Sigma_1$ be the respective extensions of τ and σ as in the proof of Proposition 2.10. By Proposition 2.10, T_1^+ is an extension of T_2 and T_2^+ is an extension of T_1. Before proceeding further, we state a brief lemma. (Note that this lemma is distinct from Lemma 2.9, since it relates each definitional extension to the 'other' translation.)

Lemma 2.15 For any $(\Sigma_1 \cup \Sigma_2)$-formula $\phi(x_1, \ldots, x_n)$,

$$T_1^+ \vDash \forall x_1 \ldots \forall x_n (\phi \leftrightarrow \tau^+\phi) \tag{2.13a}$$
$$T_2^+ \vDash \forall x_1 \ldots \forall x_n (\phi \leftrightarrow \sigma^+\phi) \tag{2.13b}$$

Proof First, for any atomic Σ_1-formula ϕ_1, $T_1 \vDash \forall x_1 \ldots \forall x_n (\phi_1 \leftrightarrow \sigma\tau\phi_1)$ by virtue of (2.12a); therefore $T_1^+ \vDash \forall x_1 \ldots \forall x_n (\phi_1 \leftrightarrow \sigma^+\tau^+\phi_1)$, and so $T_1^+ \vDash \forall x_1 \ldots \forall x_n (\phi_1 \leftrightarrow \tau^+\phi_1)$ by Lemma 2.9. Second, for any atomic Σ_2-formula ϕ_2, $(\tau^+\phi_2) \equiv \phi_2$, so trivially $T_1^+ \vDash \forall x_1 \ldots \forall x_n (\phi_2 \leftrightarrow \tau^+\phi_2)$. From there, induction on the complexity of formulae suffices to demonstrate (2.13a). The proof of (2.13b) is similar.

We want to show that T_1^+ and T_2^+ are logically equivalent. So suppose that for some $(\Sigma_1 \cup \Sigma_2)$-sentence ϕ, $T_2^+ \vDash \phi$. Then by Lemma 2.9, $T_2^+ \vDash \tau^+\phi$. Since $\tau^+\phi$ is a Σ_2-sentence and T_2^+ a conservative extension of T_2, we have that $T_2 \vDash \tau^+\phi$. Since σ is a translation from T_2 to T_1, $T_1 \vDash \sigma\tau^+\phi$, and so $T_1^+ \vDash \sigma^+\tau^+\phi$. Hence, by Lemmas 2.9 and 2.15, $T_1^+ \vDash \phi$. The proof in the other direction is similar.

In general, if we have a theory T_1, then its image $\tau[T_1]$ under a dictionary-induced map $\tau : \text{Form}(\Sigma_1) \rightarrow \text{Form}(\Sigma_2)$ is not intertranslatable with T_1.[30] However, if τ is invertible in a sense *stronger* than that given by Definition 2.13, then this does hold. More precisely:

---

[30] See Barrett and Halvorson (2016a).

Proposition 2.16 Suppose that the translations $\tau : T_1 \to T_2$ and $\sigma : T_2 \to T_1$ are such that for any Σ_1-formula $\phi(x_1, \ldots, x_n)$ and Σ_2-formula $\psi(y_1, \ldots, y_m)$,

$$\sigma[T_2] \vDash \forall x_1 \ldots \forall x_n (\phi \leftrightarrow \sigma\tau\phi) \tag{2.14a}$$

$$\tau[T_1] \vDash \forall y_1 \ldots \forall y_m (\psi \leftrightarrow \tau\sigma\psi) \tag{2.14b}$$

Then T_2 is logically equivalent to $\tau[T_1]$, and T_1 is logically equivalent to $\sigma[T_2]$.

Proof By the definition of a translation, $T_2 \vDash \tau[T_1]$ and $T_1 \vDash \sigma[T_2]$.[31] Now consider any $\psi \in T_2$; we then have that $T_1 \vDash \sigma\psi$. So for any model B of $\tau[T_1]$, $\tau^*(B) \vDash T_1$; so $\tau^*(B) \vDash \sigma\psi$; so $B \vDash \tau\sigma\psi$; so $B \vDash \psi$ (by (2.14b)). Hence, $\tau[T_1] \vDash T_2$. The proof that $\sigma[T_2] \vDash T_1$ is similar.

In particular, take as given some Σ_1-theory T_1, and suppose that $\tau :$ Form$(\Sigma_1) \to$ Form(Σ_2) and $\sigma :$ Form$(\Sigma_2) \to$ From(Σ_1) are induced by dictionaries. If $\sigma\tau\phi$ is logically equivalent to ϕ and $\tau\sigma\psi$ is logically equivalent to ψ, for every $\phi \in$ Form(Σ_1) and $\psi \in$ Form(Σ_2), then T_1 is intertranslatable with $\tau[T_1]$.

Finally, we observe that intertranslatability is associated with codetermination between models in a natural way.

Proposition 2.17 If $\tau : T_1 \to T_2$ and $\sigma : T_2 \to T_1$ are inverse translations, then:

- for any A $\in$ Mod(T_1), A is codeterminate with $\sigma^*(A)$, and $\tau^*(\sigma^*(A)) = A$; and
- for any B $\in$ Mod(T_2), B is codeterminate with $\tau^*(B)$, and $\sigma^*(\tau^*(B)) = B$.

Proof Left as exercise.

Again, there is a great deal more to be said about the concept of translation. In particular, just as there is a generalised notion of definition that enables one to define new sorts, so there is a generalised notion of translation that enables one to translate between theories that (intuitively speaking) traffic in different sorts.[32] The relationship between generalised definition and generalised translation is broadly similar to that between definition and translation, although only over the domain of so-called *proper* theories (those for which there is some formula such that the theory entails both that some object satisfies the

---

[31] This also makes clear why the condition (2.12) is stronger than (2.14).

[32] See Halvorson (2019, §5.4); a similar notion, although for single-sorted theories, is discussed in Button and Walsh (2018), chapter 5.

formula and that some object does not satisfy it).[33] However, we have said enough for our purposes, and so we move on to our next topic: that of *Ramsey sentences*.

3 Ramsey Sentences

We've now seen some of the ways in which we can use the resources of model theory to articulate different senses of equivalence between models and theories. In so doing, we have been able to indirectly shed light on the notion of structure. But as discussed in the introduction, one can turn things around: rather than using equivalences to reveal structure, we can seek to articulate a notion of 'structure' directly, and then use that to formulate a criterion of equivalence. In this section, we consider one well-known proposal for the 'structural content' of a theory: that this content can be identified with the theory's *Ramsey sentence*.[34] As we will see, however, the criterion of equivalence that this induces leaves much to be desired.

3.1 Second-order logic

As we shall see, the Ramsey sentence of a first-order theory is a second-order sentence; so we begin by reviewing the formalism of second-order logic. In second-order logic, we can – as people say – *quantify into predicate position*. Intuitively, this means that we can make quantified claims about properties (and relations): so rather than being limited to saying things like 'all whales are mammals', we can now say things like 'anything which is true of all mammals is true of all whales', or 'there are some properties which whales and dolphins both have'.

More formally, then, second-order logic is distinguished from first-order logic by having not only a stock Var of first-order variables $x, y, z, \ldots$, but also a stock VAR of second-order variables $X, Y, Z, \ldots$. Like predicates, every second-order variable has an associated arity $n \in \mathbb{N}$. And as with predicates, we will indicate the arity of a second-order variable (where helpful) by a parenthesised superscript, thus: $X^{(n)}$. The subset of VAR containing all the n-ary variables will be denoted VAR^n.

Other than this, the symbolic vocabulary of second-order logic is the same as that of first-order logic: we have the equality-symbol, the logical connectives,

---

[33] See Washington (2018), Halvorson (2019), §7.5.

[34] The Ramsey sentence was originally introduced in Ramsey (1931), although Russell (1927) contains closely related ideas. The interpretation of the Ramsey sentence as giving a theory's structural content is originally due to Maxwell (1968; 1970; 1971), but has also been defended by, for instance, Zahar (2001, 2004) and Worrall (2007). For more on the relationship between the Ramsey sentence and structural realism, see Frigg and Votsis (2011).

the quantifiers, and a signature Σ consisting of predicates (of various arities). The rules for forming well-formed formulae are the same as for first-order logic, but with two additional clauses:

- If $X^{(n)} \in$ VAR, and if $x_1, \ldots, x_n \in$ Var, then $X x_1 \ldots x_n$ is a formula.
- If ψ is a formula, and $X \in$ VAR, then $\forall X \psi$ and $\exists X \psi$ are formulas.

Respectively, these clauses tell us that the new variables can go into predicate position, and that they can be quantified over.

We now turn to the standard semantics of second-order logic.[35] We evaluate second-order sentences over the same Tarski models as were used for evaluating first-order sentences: that is, for signature Σ, a Σ-model A consists of a set A equipped with extensions for all predicates in Σ. Given a Σ-model A, a *second-order variable-assignment G* for A consists of a map $g :$ Var $\rightarrow |A|$, and for every $n \in \mathbb{N}$, a map $G^n :$ VAR$^n \rightarrow \mathcal{P}(|A|^n)$. Here, $\mathcal{P}(|A|^n)$ is the *power set* of $|A|^n$, i.e. the set containing all subsets of $|A|^n$; thus, for any $X^{(n)} \in$ VAR, $G^n(X)$ is some set of n-tuples from $|A|$.

Now let ϕ be some second-order Σ-formula, let A be a Σ-model, and let G be a second-order variable-assignment. Truth is then defined as for the first-order case, but with two extra clauses (corresponding to the two new clauses for formulae):

- For any $X^{(n)} \in$ VAR and any $x_1, \ldots, x_n \in$ Var,

$$\text{A} \models_G X x_1 \ldots x_n \text{ iff } \langle g(x_1), \ldots, g(x_n) \rangle \in G^n(X) \tag{3.1}$$

- $\text{A} \models_G \forall X^{(n)} \phi$ iff for all $A \subseteq |A|^n$, $\text{A} \models_{G_A^X} \phi$

where the variable-assignment G_A^X is defined by the condition that

$$G_A^X(Y) = \begin{cases} G(Y) & \text{if } Y \neq X \\ A & \text{if } Y = X \end{cases} \tag{3.2}$$

We then say that a sentence ϕ is true relative to a structure A if, for every variable-assignment G over A, $\text{A} \models_G \phi$. In this case, we write $\text{A} \models \phi$.

In (standard) second-order logic, various familiar first-order results cease to hold – including, for example, the Löwenheim-Skolem and Compactness Theorems. Perhaps more pertinently for our purposes, Beth's theorem (Theorem 1.17) also fails: so implicit definability need not entail explicit definability. On the other hand, it was noted that syntactic conservation does not entail semantic conservation in the first-order case; in second-order logic, these two

---

[35] See Shapiro (1991), §4.2, Manzano (1996), or Button and Walsh (2018), chapter 1, for more detailed treatments.

notions coincide.[36] Hence, we now distinguish between first-order syntactic conservation and second-order syntactic conservation; in the interest of brevity, we'll just refer to these as *first-order conservation* and *second-order conservation*.

3.2 Ramseyfication

We can now turn our attention to the Ramsey sentence itself. The intuitive idea is that the 'structural core' of a theory T will make the same structural claims about the world as T, but without committing itself to which properties or relations it is that instantiate that structure. Thus, if a theory says something like 'positively charged particles repel one another', the structural claim thereby expressed is merely 'there is a property, such that any two particles possessing that property will repel one another'. One might object that even this does not go far enough, since it still speaks of 'repulsion'; or, one might distinguish between charge and repulsion on the basis that the notion of repulsion, unlike that of positive charge, is associated with a direct empirical content. In the first instance we will take the latter attitude, since the former (more extreme) view can be recovered as a special case.

Thus suppose that our non-logical vocabulary Σ is divided into two classes, Ω and Θ: intuitively speaking, we suppose that Ω is the collection of 'observational' predicates (like 'repulsion'), while Θ is the collection of 'theoretical' predicates (like 'positive charge'). Suppose further that the theory T we are interested in (which is formulated in Σ) consists only of finitely many sentences; without loss of generality, we can suppose that T consists of a single sentence.[37] The Ramsey sentence is defined as follows.

Definition 3.1 We first form a 'skeleton' theory T^*, by replacing all the theoretical predicates that occur in T by second-order variables (of the appropriate arity): that is, if only $Q_1, \ldots, Q_p \in \Theta$ occur in T, then

---

[36] For a proof, see Button and Walsh (2018), Proposition 3.5. Intuitively, the reason for the change is that syntactic conservation is a rather stronger condition in the second-order context, owing to the added expressive power of the language.

[37] In principle, we could apply the Ramseyfication procedure to a theory which consisted of infinitely many sentences. However, we would need the second-order language of T^R to be an *infinitary* second-order language: if T contained κ-many sentences, and if λ-many predicates from Θ occur in T, then T^R must be in a language that permits κ-size conjunction, and which admits the introduction of λ-many second-order quantifiers. In order to not have to deal with these complications, we will suppose that the original theory is finite.

$$T^* = T[X_1/Q_1, \ldots, X_p/Q_p] \qquad (3.3)$$

where for each i, X_i is of the same arity as Q_i. We then form the *Ramsey sentence* of T by existentially quantifying over all of these predicates:

$$T^R = \exists X_1 \exists X_2 \ldots \exists X_p T^* \qquad (3.4)$$

We will take the signature of the Ramsey sentence to be Ω.

We can now ask the question: how much of a theory's structure does the Ramsey sentence capture? To answer this question, it is helpful to compare the models of the original theory with the models of its Ramsey sentence. We then have the following result, which states that the models of the Ramsey sentence are precisely the Ω-reducts of the models of the original theory – equivalently, that the original theory is a semantically conservative extension of its Ramsey sentence.[38]

Proposition 3.2 For any Ω-model A, A $\models T^R$ iff for some expansion A^+ of A to Σ, $A^+ \models T$.

Proof If A $\models T^R$, then there is some second-order variable-assignment G for A such that A $\models_G T^*$. Now define a Σ-model A^+ as follows:

$$|A^+| = |A|$$
$$P^{A^+} = P^A, \text{ for every } P \in \Omega$$
$$Q_i^{A^+} = G(X_i), \text{ for every } Q_i \in \Theta$$

A proof by induction shows that $A^+ \models T$.

In the other direction, suppose that $A^+ \models T$, for some expansion A^+ of A. Then $A^+ \models_G T^*$, where $G(X_i) = Q_i$ for every $Q_i \in \Theta$; and hence $A^+ \models T^R$. But since T^R is an Ω-sentence, A $\models T^R$.

Corollary 3.3 Let S be any Ω-theory (and T be any Σ-theory). Then $S \models T^R$ iff T is semantically conservative over S.

It follows that if $S \models T^R$, then T is first-order conservative over S. As mentioned at the end of the previous subsection, second-order conservation is

---

[38] This way of characterising the Ramsey sentence's content is due to Button and Walsh (2018): as they put it, it suggests thinking of Ramsey sentences as 'object-language statements of conservation' (p. 62).

equivalent to semantic conservation: so we also have that for any Ω-theory S, $S \vDash T^R$ iff T is second-order conservative over S.[39]

Proposition 3.2 also lets us prove a key result about Ramsey sentences: that they suffice to prove the observational consequences of the original theory.

Proposition 3.4 Let ϕ be any (first- or second-order) sentences of signature Ω. If $T \vDash \phi$, then $T^R \vDash \phi$.

Proof Suppose that $T \vDash \phi$ yet $T^R \nvDash \phi$. Then for some Ω-model A, A $\vDash T^R$ and A $\nvDash \phi$. By Proposition 3.2, there is an expansion A^+ of A such that $A^+ \vDash T$; hence, $A^+ \vDash \phi$. But since ϕ is an Ω-sentence, it follows that A $\vDash \phi$. So by contradiction, the result follows.

Thus let T_Ω^{FOL} be the Ω-theory consisting of all first-order Ω-consequences of T: that is, of all first-order Ω-sentences ϕ such that $T \vDash \phi$. And let T_Ω^{SOL} be Ω-theory consisting of all second-order Ω-consequences of T: that is, of all second-order Ω-sentences ϕ such that $T \vDash \phi$. By construction, T is second-order conservative over T_Ω^{SOL} and first-order conservative over T_Ω^{FOL}. Then by Proposition 3.4, $T_\Omega^{\text{FOL}} = (T^R)_\Omega^{\text{FOL}}$ and $T_\Omega^{\text{SOL}} = (T^R)_\Omega^{\text{SOL}}$; hence, $T^R \vDash T_\Omega^{\text{FOL}}$ and $T^R \vDash T_\Omega^{\text{SOL}}$. Moreover, by Corollary 3.3, $T_\Omega^{\text{SOL}} \vDash T^R$, and so T^R and T_Ω^{SOL} are logically equivalent. However, in general, $T_\Omega^{\text{FOL}} \nvDash T^R$.

We can now use these formal results to indicate the potential problem with using the Ramsey sentence as an encapsulation of a theory's structural content. First, define the *observational reduct* of any Σ-model A to be its reduct $A|_\Omega$ to Ω. Second, let W be a Σ-model which is a faithful representation of the world: i.e. which has the observational and theoretical predicates distributed over its elements in just the way that the corresponding observational and theoretical properties are distributed over the objects of the world.[40] We'll say that a Σ-theory is *true* if W is one of its models; that it is *observationally adequate* if it has some model whose observational reduct is identical to $W|_\Omega$; and that it is *numerically adequate* if it has some model whose domain coincides with $|W|$. Intuitively, a theory which is true admits a model which matches the actual number of objects, and the actual distribution of observational and theoretical properties over those objects; a theory which is observationally adequate admits a model which matches the actual number of objects, and the actual distribution of observational properties over those objects; and a theory which

---

[39] Compare this with Button and Walsh (2018), Proposition 3.5.
[40] If this formulation makes you uncomfortable (which it probably should), then just think of W as a 'preferred model', without worrying about in virtue of what it is preferred.

is numerically adequate admits a model which matches the actual number of objects.[41]

This enables us to now make the following observation: for any Σ-theory T, its Ramsey sentence T^R is true just in case T is observationally adequate.[42] More formally, the result below follows immediately from Proposition 3.2:

Proposition 3.5 Let T be a theory of signature Σ. Then $\mathsf{W}|_\Omega \models T^R$ if and only if T is observationally adequate (i.e. there is some model A of T such that $\mathsf{A}|_\Omega = \mathsf{W}|_\Omega$).

We also have the following corollary, which applies to the more radical view canvassed above (that the use of *all* predicates, not just the 'theoretical' ones, should be converted to existential quantifications).

Corollary 3.6 Suppose that $\Theta = \varnothing$ (equivalently, that $\Sigma = \Omega$); that is, consider the case where we Ramsefy away *all* the vocabulary. Then $\mathsf{W} \models T^R$ if and only if T is numerically adequate (i.e. there is some model A of T such that $|\mathsf{A}| = |\mathsf{W}|$).

Philosophically, this observation is often presented as a problem – known as *Newman's objection* – for the proposal that a theory's structure is captured by its Ramsey sentence: simply put, the concern is that Proposition 3.5 shows that the Ramsey sentence fails to capture anything about a theory beyond its empirical or observational content.[43] So if we do indeed take the 'structure' of a theory to be that which is captured by its Ramsey sentence, then we appear to have the corollary that a theory simply has no non-observational structure. Moreover, there is something faintly paradoxical to this, insofar as the observational predicates were precisely the ones that we did not Ramseyfy. So the Ramsey-sentence approach to structure seems to hold that although the Ramsey sentence of a theory articulates that theory's structure, the only structure a theory in fact possesses is expressed by that part of the theory's language which is not subject to Ramseyfication!

---

[41] Bear in mind here that W is merely supposed to be a 'faithful representative' of the world, not 'the world itself' (whatever, exactly, these terms might mean). So it's harmless to define observational adequacy as the theory admitting a model identical to W_Ω (not just isomorphic to it), and to define numerical adequacy as the theory admitting a model with a domain identical to $|\mathsf{W}|$ (not just equinumerous with it).

[42] Compare Ketland (2004), Theorem 2.

[43] The objection is so-called because a version of it was discussed in Newman (1928). Note that this is *before* the introduction of the Ramsey sentence in Ramsey (1931) – even allowing for the fact that Ramsey's essay was written in 1929. The reason for this is that Newman's objection was, originally, offered as a criticism of Russell (1927), and only later applied to the Ramsey-sentence approach to theories. Its application to debates on structural realism was in Demopoulos and Friedman (1985).

3.3 Ramsey equivalence

If the Ramsey sentence is taken as expressing a theory's structure, then it is natural to take two theories as equivalent if they have logically equivalent Ramsey sentences. A further way of thinking about Newman's objection is to observe that, if we use standard second-order semantics, then this criterion of equivalence degenerates into a form of observational equivalence. More precisely, we give the following definitions.

Definition 3.7 Two Σ-theories T_1 and T_2 are *Ramsey equivalent* if they have logically equivalent Ramsey sentences.

Definition 3.8 Two Σ-theories T_1 and T_2 are *semantically observationally equivalent* iff the observational reducts of their models coincide: that is, if for every model A of T_1, there is some model B of T_2 such that $A|_\Omega = B|_\Omega$, and vice versa.

Definition 3.9 Two Σ-theories T_1 and T_2 are *second-order observationally equivalent* iff their second-order observational consequences coincide: that is, if $(T_1)^{SOL}_\Omega = (T_2)^{SOL}_\Omega$.

In light of what has been said already, it is not hard to show that these notions of equivalence all coincide with one another:

Proposition 3.10 Two theories are Ramsey equivalent iff they are semantically observationally equivalent iff they are second-order observationally equivalent.

Proof Left as exercise.

What can be said in response? One option is to bite the bullet, and argue that – in fact – it is *good* that a theory's structure should turn out to be exhausted by its observational structure. In other words, the Ramsey sentence can be regarded as a useful vehicle for expressing a (fairly strong) form of empiricism about scientific theories: it offers one way of making precise the idea that the real content of a scientific theory is its observational or empirical 'core'. This is, roughly speaking, the attitude that Carnap (1958) took in advocating the Ramsey sentence as expressing the 'synthetic part' of a theory, with the 'analytic part' expressed by the so-called *Carnap sentence*, $T^C = (T^R \to T)$.[44]

---

[44] For commentary and discussion, see Psillos (2000) or Andreas (2017).

For non-empiricists, it is less clear what the best response is.[45] One option is to argue that realism requires a commitment only to the idea that theories which have the same *first-order* observational consequences could, nevertheless, be inequivalent; one can then appeal to the fact that Ramsey equivalence is strictly stronger than this criterion of observational equivalence. That is, we have the following:

Definition 3.11 Two Σ-theories T_1 and T_2 are *first-order observationally equivalent* iff their first-order observational consequences coincide: that is, if $(T_1)^{\text{FOL}}_{\Omega} = (T_2)^{\text{FOL}}_{\Omega}$.

Proposition 3.12 First-order observational equivalence is strictly weaker than the other forms of observational equivalence: two theories can be first-order observationally equivalent without being semantically observationally equivalent (or Ramsey equivalent, or second-order observationally equivalent).

Proof Let T_1 be a Σ-theory and T_2 an Ω-theory, such that T_1 is first-order conservative over T_2 but not semantically conservative over T_2; Proposition 1.18 guarantees that this assumption is permissible. Then by construction, T_1 and T_2 are first-order observationally equivalent. If they were semantically observationally equivalent, then for every model B of T_2, there would be some model A of T_1 such that $A|_{\Omega} = B$ (since $B|_{\Omega} = B$). But this is just to say that T_1 is semantically conservative over T_2, which we assumed was not the case. So in general, it is not the case that first-order observational equivalence entails semantic observational equivalence.

However, this move seems somewhat *ad hoc*. Indeed, the fact that semantic observational equivalence and second-order observational equivalence coincide lends credence to the idea that this is the more 'natural' criterion of observational equivalence. Such judgments are obviously subjective, but it feels to me that first-order observational equivalence ends up being weaker primarily as a result of the expressive shortcomings of first-order logic.

An alternative is to argue that the way we have formalised the Ramsey sentence failed to capture the intuitive idea. In particular, note that our intuitive gloss above quantified over *properties*, whereas the standard semantics for second-order logic permits the second-order variables to range over *arbitrary subsets of the domain*. So one might argue that the Ramsey-sentence

---

[45] To be clear, there are other 'realist' responses available beyond that discussed here: see Button and Walsh (2018), chapter 3, for a deeper dive into what further moves and counter-moves are available.

approach to structural content should use some other semantics for second-order logic, where the range of the second-order quantifiers is somehow restricted.

A natural way of doing this is to use so-called *Henkin semantics*. In a *Henkin model* H, for each $n \in \mathbb{N}$ a subset of $\mathcal{P}(|H|^n)$ is picked out as the permitted range for the second-order n-ary variables to range over.[46] This can be shown to avoid the Newman objection; however, it turns out that this still captures a relatively weak notion of structural content, as the following proposition indicates.

Proposition 3.13 If T_1 and T_2 are mutually translatable (in the sense of Definition 2.11), then their Ramsey sentences are logically equivalent under Henkin semantics.

Proof See Dewar (2019a).

As Example 2.12 showed, mutual translatability is already a fairly weak notion of equivalence, so it is problematic to have that as a sufficient condition for equivalence.

Overall, then, the notions of equivalence that we get out of considering the Ramsey sentence are not – it turns out – very promising. Next, we look at a rather different way of isolating the 'structural content' of theories: by using tools from *category theory*.

4 Categories of Theories

We have now met various tools for establishing precise ideas concerning structure and equivalence in the context of logic: definitions, translations, and Ramsey sentences. This section (the last 'pure logic' section of this Element) discusses the use of one final tool: *category theory*. Familiarity with the basic concepts of category, functor, and categorical equivalence will be assumed.[47]

4.1 Categories of Tarski Models

In the previous sections, we considered the concept of a class of models of a first-order theory. However, for many purposes, it is helpful to work with the richer concept of a *category* of models.[48]

---

[46] Moreover, we require that these privileged subsets are, in an appropriate sense, closed under definability; see Manzano (1996) for details.

[47] For introductions to category theory, see for example van Oosten (2002) or Awodey (2010).

[48] The ideas in this subsection are covered in much greater detail in Halvorson (2019).

Definition 4.1 Given a theory T, the *category of models* of T is a category $\text{Mod}(T)$ whose objects are models of T and whose arrows are elementary embeddings.

Elementary embeddings are not the only kinds of mappings between models that are considered in model theory: there are also, for example, homomorphisms and embeddings.[49] So why do we choose elementary embeddings to be the arrows in our category of models? The reason is that if we do so, then translations between theories induce functors between their categories of models:

Proposition 4.2 Given theories T_1 and T_2, let $\text{Mod}(T_1)$ and $\text{Mod}(T_2)$ be their categories of models. If $\tau : T_1 \rightarrow T_2$ is a translation, then τ^* is extendable to a functor, by stipulating that for any elementary embedding $h : A \rightarrow B$ (where A, B are objects of $\text{Mod}(T_2)$), $\tau^*(h) = h$.

Proof Suppose that $\tau^*(h)$, i.e. h, is not an elementary embedding of $\tau^*(A)$ into $\tau^*(B)$: that is, that there is some Σ_1-formula $\phi(x_1, \ldots, x_n)$ and some $a_1, \ldots, a_n \in |A|$ such that $\tau^*(A) \models \phi[a_1, \ldots, a_n]$ but $\tau^*(B) \not\models \phi[h(a_1), \ldots, h(a_n)]$. It follows that $A \models \tau(\phi)[a_1, \ldots, a_n]$, and $B \not\models \tau(\phi)[h(a_1), \ldots, a_n]$; so h is not an elementary embedding of A into B. Thus, given an elementary embedding h in $\text{Mod}(T_2)$, $\tau^*(h)$ is an elementary embedding in $\text{Mod}(T_1)$. Since $\tau^*(h) = h$, it is guaranteed to preserve composition and identities; hence τ^* is a functor.

Had we taken homomorphisms or embeddings as arrows, this would not hold true, as the following examples demonstrate.

Example 4.3 Consider the following theories, T_1 and T_2. T_1 has signature $\{P\}$, and axioms

$$\exists x \exists y (x \neq y \wedge \forall z (z = x \vee z = y)) \tag{4.1a}$$

$$\exists x P x \tag{4.1b}$$

while T_2 has signature $\{Q\}$ and axioms

$$\exists x \exists y (x \neq y \wedge \forall z (z = x \vee z = y)) \tag{4.2a}$$

---

[49] Recall that a *homomorphism* $h : A \rightarrow B$ is a map $h : |A| \rightarrow |B|$ such that for any $R^{(n)} \in \Sigma$ and any $a_1, \ldots, a_n \in |A|$, if $\langle a_1, \ldots, a_n \rangle \in R$ then $\langle h(a_1), \ldots, h(a_n) \rangle \in R$; an embedding is a map $h : |A| \rightarrow |B|$ such that for any $R^{(n)} \in \Sigma$ and any $a_1, \ldots, a_n \in |A|$, $\langle a_1, \ldots, a_n \rangle \in R$ iff $\langle h(a_1), \ldots, h(a_n) \rangle \in R$; and an elementary embedding is an embedding $h : A \rightarrow B$ such that for any Σ-formula ϕ and any $a_1, \ldots, a_n \in |A|$, $A \models \phi[a_1, \ldots, a_n]$ iff $B \models \phi[h(a_1), \ldots, h(a_n)]$.

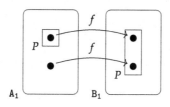

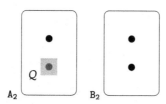

Figure 7 The models of the theories in Example 4.3

$$\exists x \neg Q x \tag{4.2b}$$

Figure 7 displays the models of these theories: the models of T_1 are A_1 and B_1, and the models of T_2 are A_2 and B_2.

The map

$$Qx \mapsto \neg Px \tag{4.3}$$

is a translation from T_2 to T_1; the associated semantic map will map A_1 to A_2 and B_1 to B_2. But there is a homomorphism from A_1 to B_1 (labelled as f on Figure 7) yet no homomorphisms from A_2 to B_2; so there can be no functor from the category of models of T_1 with homomorphisms as arrows to the category of models of T_2 with homomorphisms as arrows.

Example 4.4 Let T_1 be the theory in signature $\{P^{(1)}\}$ with the following axioms:

$$\exists x \exists y (\forall z (z = x \lor z = y)) \tag{4.4}$$

$$\exists x (Px \land \forall y (Py \rightarrow y = x)) \tag{4.5}$$

Let T_2 be the theory in signature $\{Q^{(1)}\}$ with the following axioms:

$$\exists x \exists y (\forall z (z = x \lor z = y)) \tag{4.6}$$

$$(\exists y \exists z (y \neq z) \leftrightarrow \forall x Q x) \tag{4.7}$$

The models of T_1 and T_2 are depicted and labelled in Figure 8.

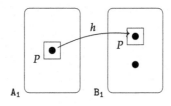

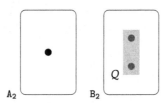

Figure 8 The models of the theories in Example 4.4

The map

$$Qx \mapsto (x = x \wedge \exists z \neg Pz) \tag{4.8}$$

is a translation from T_2 to T_1. However, although there is an embedding h from A_1 to B_1, there are no embeddings from A_2 to B_2; hence there can be no functor from the category of models of T_1 with embeddings as arrows to the category of models of T_2 with embeddings as arrows.

4.2 Categories and Definability

Thus we take the category of models of a theory to be one with elementary embeddings as arrows. We have already seen that invertible translations induce bijective maps on models; since the extension of such a map to a functor just acts as the identity on elementary embeddings, it follows more or less immediately that the functor is an isomorphism between the categories of models—and hence that it is an equivalence. Thus, intertranslatability entails categorical equivalence. In the other direction, however, categorical equivalence does *not* entail intertranslatability (see Barrett and Halvorson, 2016b, theorem 5.7).

What about mutual translatability? On the one hand, mutual translatability does not entail categorical equivalence.

Example 4.5 Consider again the theories T_1 and T_2 from Example 2.12:

$$T_1 = \{\exists x \forall y (y = x)\} \tag{4.9}$$

$$T_2 = \{\exists x \forall y (y = x), \forall x Px\} \tag{4.10}$$

where both theories are in signature $\{P^{(1)}\}$. Although mutually translatable, these theories are not categorically equivalent. For, up to isomorphism, T_1 has two models whereas T_2 has only one, and so any functor $F : \text{Mod}(T_1) \to \text{Mod}(T_2)$ cannot be full: it would have to map the empty set of morphisms between T_1's models to the non-empty set of morphisms from T_2's sole model to itself.

On the other hand, categorical equivalence does not entail mutual translatability – nor, in fact, does it entail the existence of a translation in either direction.[50] (This example also serves to demonstrate that categorical equivalence does not entail intertranslatability.)

Example 4.6 Consider the following two theories. T_1 has the empty signature, and as its sole axiom

$$\exists x \forall y (y = x) \tag{4.11}$$

T_2 has signature $\{P^{(1)}\}$ and axioms

$$\exists x \exists y (x \neq y \wedge \forall z(z = x \vee z = y)) \tag{4.12}$$

$$\exists x P x \wedge \exists x \neg P x \tag{4.13}$$

Up to isomorphism, T_1 and T_2 each have a unique model: the unique model A_1 of T_1 has one element, while the unique model A_2 of T_2 has two elements, of which exactly one is P. Since neither model has any non-trivial automorphisms, the categories $\text{Mod}(T_1)$ and $\text{Mod}(T_2)$ are discrete – and so, trivially, they are categorically equivalent. But since any translation from T_1 to T_2 would have to map A_2 onto a model of T_1 with an equinumerous domain, there can be no such translation, and the same is true in the other direction. Hence there are no translations between T_1 and T_2 (and hence T_1 and T_2 are not mutually translatable).

The result, therefore, is that categorical equivalence and mutual translatability are independent of one another: they represent distinct ways to weaken the condition of intertranslatability.

Rather than merely comparing equivalence criteria based on definability to those based on category theory, however, it is more instructive to think about ways of *combining* the two. In particular, what happens if we *stipulate* that we will be interested only in categorical equivalences that are suitably associated with translations? To that end, let us say (given theories T_1 and T_2) that a functor

---

[50] I'm grateful to an anonymous referee for suggesting this example.

F : $\text{Mod}(T_2)$ → $\text{Mod}(T_1)$ is a *translation functor* if there is a translation $\tau : T_1 \rightarrow T_2$ such that $F = \tau^*$. It turns out that categorical equivalence *by a translation functor* is sufficient for intertranslatability.

Definition 4.7 Two theories T_1 and T_2 are *translationally categorically equivalent* iff there is a translation $\tau : T_1 \rightarrow T_2$ such that $\tau^* : \text{Mod}(T_2) \rightarrow \text{Mod}(T_1)$ is an equivalence functor.[51]

Proposition 4.8 If T_1 and T_2 are translationally categorically equivalent, then T_1 and T_2 are intertranslatable.

Proof See Barrett and Halvorson, n.d., proposition 6.

Since a pair of inverse translations will (as we have seen) induce a categorical equivalence, and that equivalence will by definition be a translation functor, we see that intertranslatability is equivalent to translational categorical equivalence.

In Sections 1 and 2, it was remarked that there exist generalisations of the notion of definition and translation that enable one to define new sorts. How do these relate to categorical equivalence (where the categories are, again, taken to be categories of models with elementary embeddings as arrows)? First, one can show that if a pair of theories are Morita equivalent, i.e. weakly intertranslatable, then they are categorically equivalent via a functor induced by a generalised translation.[52] Second, (mere) categorical equivalence does not entail Morita equivalence.[53] Finally, to the best of my knowledge, there is not (as yet) an analogue of Proposition 4.8, nor a counterexample: so it remains an open question whether categorical equivalence via a generalised translation functor entails Morita equivalence.

This wraps up our analysis of structure and equivalence in logical theories. For those struggling to keep track, the relationships between the different notions of equivalence that have been discussed are laid out in Figure 9. We turn now to how these questions play out in physical contexts, by a detailed examination of two case studies. The first case study is the theory of *Newtonian mechanics*.

---

[51] This is related to but slightly stronger than Hudetz's notion of *definable categorical equivalence* (Hudetz, 2019): Hudetz is working in a higher-order context, and his 'reconstruction manuals' are permitted to define new types (making them closer to the 'generalised translations' discussed briefly at the end of Section 2).

[52] Barrett and Halvorson (2016b). Furthermore, this result can be extended to the case of higher-order theories: see Hudetz (2019).

[53] (Barrett and Halvorson, 2016b, theorem 5.7)

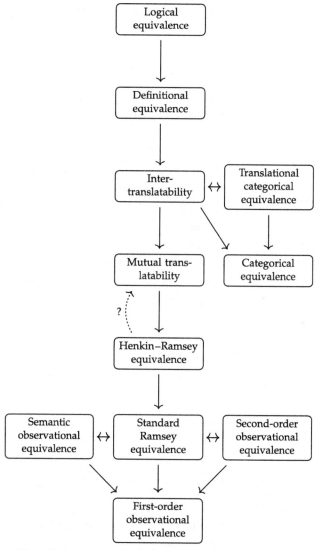

Figure 9 The relations of equivalence discussed in the preceding sections. Arrows indicate the relative strength of these relations; the dotted arrow from Henkin–Ramsey equivalence to mutual translatability indicates that it is not known whether this entailment holds or not.

5 Newtonian Mechanics

Having looked at various formal notions of structure and equivalence, we now shift our attention to some more robustly physical examples. Our first example will be that of classical N-particle Newtonian mechanics. I will begin by introducing the theory, in a coordinate-based form. Next, we will consider in what ways we can regard this theory as analogous to the theories that we dealt with in the previous sections. Finally, we will consider the analogue of translations for a theory such as this: *changes of variables*.

5.1 Newtonian Mechanics in Coordinates

We take as given a coordinate system with x-, y-, and z-axes, which persists over time; and we take as given some clock that measures the passage of time. We label our N particles by indices n, p, and so forth. We use the variable t to represent time. We use variables x_n^1, x_n^2, and x_n^3 to represent the x-, y-, and z-components of the nth particle's position; its mass will be represented by m_n, and the x-, y-, and z-components of the net force on it will be represented by F_n^1, F_n^2, and F_n^3, respectively. We'll use i, j, and so on as indices ranging from 1 to 3, so that we write x_n^i, F_n^j, and so forth.

All of the above variables are assumed to be real-valued, i.e. to take values in (copies of) the real numbers $\mathbb{R}$. Where we have tuples of variables, such as (x_n^1, x_n^2, x_n^3), we will regard those tuples as taking values in Cartesian powers of $\mathbb{R}$ (such as in $\mathbb{R}^3$, in this example). It will be convenient to introduce some notation for the various 'copies' of $\mathbb{R}$ in which these variables are taking values. Thus we will denote the copy of $\mathbb{R}$ in which t takes values by $\mathbb{T}$; the copy of $\mathbb{R}$ in which x_n^i takes values (for any n) by $\mathbb{X}^i$, with $\mathbb{X} := \mathbb{X}^1 \times \mathbb{X}^2 \times \mathbb{X}^3$; and the copy of $\mathbb{R}$ in which F_n^i takes values (for any n) by $\vec{\mathbb{X}}^i$, with $\vec{\mathbb{X}} := \vec{\mathbb{X}}^1 \times \vec{\mathbb{X}}^2 \times \vec{\mathbb{X}}^3$.

The *dynamical equations* for this theory are (for $1 \leq i \leq 3$ and $1 \leq n \leq N$)

$$m_n \frac{d^2 x_n^i}{dt^2} = F_n^i \tag{5.1}$$

A *model* of our theory of Newtonian mechanics consists of a specification of the masses m_n of all particles, of the time-dependent forces F_n^i on those particles, and of the time-dependent positions of those particles, in such a way that the above equations are satisfied. In more formal detail, a model consists of the following data: for each n from 1 to N, and each i from 1 to 3,

- a positive real number m_n;
- a smooth function $x_n^i : \mathbb{T} \to \mathbb{X}^i$; and
- a smooth function $F_n^i : \mathbb{T} \to \vec{\mathbb{X}}^i$

such that Eq. (5.1) is satisfied.

The above is more of a framework than a theory; we can make it more specific by stipulating force laws for the forces F_n^i. For example, if we suppose that each of our N particles has an electric charge $q_n \in \mathbb{R}$, and that they are in some electrical field given by $E : \mathbb{X} \to \vec{\mathbb{X}}$, then we have

$$F_n^i = q_n E^i(x_n) \tag{5.2}$$

On the other hand, if we are instead considering a theory where the N particles are mutually interacting through gravitation, then

$$F_n^i = \sum_{p \neq n} \frac{G m_p m_n}{|x_n - x_p|^2} \frac{x_n^i - x_p^i}{|x_n - x_p|} \tag{5.3}$$

where

$$|x_n - x_p| := \sqrt{\sum_j (x_n^j - x_p^j)^2} \tag{5.4}$$

Finally, in the trivial case of free particles, the force laws are especially simple:

$$F_n^i = 0 \tag{5.5}$$

5.2 Logic and Physics

How, then, can we relate the theory above to the apparatus developed in the previous sections? One approach is to seek to systematically rewrite the above equations in explicit logical form. In principle, this can no doubt be done, although we may well require second-order logic in order to properly capture the theory of real analysis that underpins it.[54] For our purposes, however, it will be more insightful to pursue a more direct analogy.

To motivate this analogy, begin by considering again what a model of Newtonian mechanics looks like. As just noted, it consists of N real numbers, and $6N$ real-valued functions of $\mathbb{T}$. Hence, for every $t \in \mathbb{T}$, the model specifies the value of $F_n^i(t)$ and $x_n^i(t)$ (and m_n, although this is not $\mathbb{T}$-dependent). Now consider a monadic Tarski model A, i.e. a Tarski model for a signature containing only unary predicates $P, Q, \ldots$. This model will specify, for each individual of the domain $|A|$, whether the predicates in the signature hold of that individual or not. If we regard an extension as a map from $|A|$ to $\{0, 1\}$ (i.e. if we represent subsets by their characteristic functions), then we can put this as follows: the model specifies, for each $a \in |A|$, the value of $P(a)$, $Q(a)$, and so forth.

This suggests an analogy between logical theories and our theory of Newtonian mechanics. In every model of the Newtonian theory, the role of the domain is played by $\mathbb{T}$. The analogue of a logical variable is an *independent variable*

---

[54] That said, there are ongoing research efforts to see how much of physics can be captured within a first-order formalism. See, in particular, the work of the Andréka-Németi group on first-order formulations of relativity theory: for instance, Andréka et al. (2007) and references therein.

such as t, which can range over the domain. The *dependent variables* x_n^i and F_n^i are analogous to predicates: the semantics associates these with maps from the domain to some suitable space of values. So one point of disanalogy is simply that whereas our logical theories dealt only in two-valued predicates, i.e. predicates whose semantic correlate are maps to $\{0, 1\}$, the Newtonian theory features real-valued predicates.[55]

A more significant disanalogy concerns the nature of the domain. In the logical context, the domain is taken to be a mere unstructured set; whatever structure it might possess is only endowed on it by the predicates in question. Here, however, the 'domain' $\mathbb{T}$ is a highly structured object – specifically, a complete ordered field – and it possesses this structure independently of considerations about the 'predicates' (the dependent variables). We could smooth out this wrinkle by supposing that there is an 'implicit' theory describing the structure of the domain, which we do not discuss; alternatively, we could simply take it as part of the stipulation of the semantics that a variable like t takes values in a complete ordered field rather than a mere set. (Compare the way that in second-order semantics, it is simply part of the specification of the semantics that a second-order variable takes values in the power-set of the domain, rather than a mere set.)

Either way, the fact that the domain has structure means that the syntactic resources available to the Newtonian theory are somewhat richer. For example, an expression like $x(t - t_0)$ is well-formed: that is, we can employ algebraic combinations of independent variables in formulating expressions. More significantly, perhaps, the structure of $\mathbb{T}$ enables us to use *differential* expressions. Ignoring the i's and n's for a moment, consider an expression like dx/dt. We know, of course, the mathematical definition of this expression:

$$\frac{dx}{dt}(t) := \lim_{\varepsilon \to 0} \frac{x(t + \varepsilon) - x(t)}{\varepsilon} \tag{5.6}$$

with the notion of limit to be cashed out in the standard Bolzano-Weierstrass fashion. This definition is possible because of the (presumed) structure on the domain $\mathbb{T}$: if $\mathbb{T}$ were a mere set, then we could not take limits of functions on $\mathbb{T}$ in the required fashion (nor, as just discussed, could we help ourselves to expressions like $t + \varepsilon$). Of course, the same point goes for the formulation of higher derivatives such as d^2x/dt^2.

It is also worth remarking that differential expressions refer to what we might think of as extrinsic monadic properties: properties such as 'fatherhood' which

---

[55] Although note that even within logic, one might allow predicates to take more than two values: in three-valued logics, for instance, or when working with Boolean-valued structures. For the former, see Sider (2010), chap. 3; for the latter, see Button and Walsh (2018), chap. 11.

do not supervene upon the intrinsic nature of the bearer.[56] An expression like dx/dt or d^2x/dt^2 is (the analogue of) a one-place formula, since it takes a single argument t; its definition, though, refers to points outside of the point of evaluation. That is, if we leave the value of x at t the same, but alter the values of x outside of t, then we should expect the value of dx/dt at t to change. It is therefore analogous to an expression such as $\exists y Rxy$, and (like this expression) can be taken to refer to an extrinsic monadic property. (Although as with the other 'properties' we consider, its range of values is $\mathbb{R}$, rather than the two-element set $\{0, 1\}$.)

This puts us in a position to spell out the final part of the analogy: the analogy between the dynamical equations of our Newtonian theory (such as Eq. (5.1)) and the sentences of a first-order theory. In the light of what we have already said, $d^2x_n^i/dt^2$ and F_n^i are to be regarded as analogous to one-place formulas. m_n may be regarded, correspondingly, as analogous to a sentence (which receives a fixed value in every model of the theory). For any i and n, the corresponding dynamical equation therefore asserts a relationship between these expressions – namely, that the algebraic combination $m_n \cdot d^2x_n^i/dt^2$ has, for every t, the same value as F_n^i. We may therefore think of it as a kind of universally quantified assertion.

The analogy is clearer if we imagine re-expressing a (universally quantified and monadic) first-order sentence in a more 'algebraic' fashion. For example, consider the sentence

$$\forall x((Fx \wedge Gx) \leftrightarrow (Px \vee Qx)) \tag{5.7}$$

Just like Eq. (5.1), this can be regarded as asserting a coincidence in value, for every x, between certain algebraic combinations of the predicates F, G, P, Q. To see this, let $\cdot$ and $+$ stand for the Boolean operations of conjunction and disjunction, acting on the two-element set $\{0, 1\}$ just as they would act on truth-values (with 0 as False and 1 as True).[57] Then we can rewrite (5.7) as

$$F \cdot G = P + Q \tag{5.8}$$

which more closely resembles Eq. (5.1).

To close, I note that the reader might be puzzled as to why we have not made out the analogy in a different way: namely, by taking x_n^i, and so forth, to be

---

[56] This points toward some of the problems with taking classical mechanics to be a theory that is only concerned with intrinsic properties of spacetime points, à la Lewis (1994). For more on this, see Butterfield (2006).

[57] That is, $0 \cdot 0 = 0 \cdot 1 = 1 \cdot 0 = 0$ and $1 \cdot 1 = 1$; while $1 + 1 = 1 + 0 = 0 + 1 = 1$ and $0 + 0 = 0$. (Note that $+$ is therefore not the same as arithmetic addition, which after all isn't well-defined as an operation on $\{0, 1\}$.)

analogous to function- rather than predicate symbols. After all, to make this analogy work, we have ended up having to think of properties as functions! The truth is that that way of doing the analogy would also have worked, especially at this early stage, but would actually end up making our lives more difficult later on. At this stage, all the (physical) functions we are working with can be thought of as having the same domain and range: that is, $\mathbb{R}$. So in this sense, they are like the functions that we encountered in previous sections. However, we will shortly want to interpret dependent variables in terms of functions that map between different sets. This can be handled, but it gets a bit messy: we should have to think of all the different sets as disjoint subsets of a single big domain, with different predicates labelling them, and appropriate side-conditions imposed on our functions to fix their range, and to handle the case where they take arguments outside their domain. In light of this, we have taken the path outlined in this subsection.[58]

5.3 Changes of Variables

This analogy now enables us to pick up the themes of translation and definition that we explored in the first two sections, and apply them to the idea of *theoretical equivalence* in physics. We will begin with an almost trivial species of equivalence: the equivalence between the different forms a theory takes when it is formulated in *different coordinate systems*.[59] Let's first rehearse an example of such a pair of formulations, and then see what light the notions of translation can shed on this. For the sake of simplicity, let us set $N = 1$ and suppress the third spatial dimension (along the z-axis); adopting a more compact notation where $x_1^1 = x$, $x_1^2 = y$, and dots denote differentiation with respect to t, the theory (5.1) reduces to

$$m\ddot{x} = F^x \tag{5.9a}$$

$$m\ddot{y} = F^y \tag{5.9b}$$

It will also be helpful to denote $\mathbb{X}^1$ by X, and $\mathbb{X}^2$ by Y; so a model of the theory consists of a positive real number m, a smooth function $(x, y) : \mathbb{T} \to X \times Y$, and a smooth function $(F^x, F^y) : \mathbb{T} \to \vec{X} \times \vec{Y}$.

---

[58] Plausibly the best option would have been to start with many-sorted logic, which gives a very natural way to handle functions mapping between different sets; we could then employ the generalised notions of definition and translation to cash out the analogy to physics.

[59] Although, as we will discuss in Section 8, even this case can raise some difficult interpretational questions.

We now compare this with a (prima facie) different theory: this second theory consists of the dynamical equations

$$m(\ddot{r} - r\dot{\theta}^2) = F^r \tag{5.10a}$$

$$m(2\dot{r}\dot{\theta} + r\ddot{\theta}) = rF^\theta \tag{5.10b}$$

In this theory, r denotes the radial distance from the origin; θ denotes the angle subtended between a line joining the particle to the origin and the x-axis; and F^r and F^θ denote the radial and transverse components of the force (see Figure 10).[60] Standardly, we take this latter theory (given the above interpretation of its terms) as expressing the same physical content as the theory (5.9). The relationship between the two theories is taken to be expressed by the formulae expressing changes of coordinates:

$$x = r \cos \theta \tag{5.11a}$$

$$y = r \sin \theta \tag{5.11b}$$

$$F^x = F^r \cos \theta - rF^\theta \sin \theta \tag{5.11c}$$

$$F^y = F^r \sin \theta + rF^\theta \cos \theta \tag{5.11d}$$

and

$$r = \sqrt{x^2 + y^2} \tag{5.12a}$$

$$\theta = \tan^{-1}\left(\frac{y}{x}\right) \tag{5.12b}$$

$$F^r = \frac{x}{\sqrt{x^2 + y^2}} F^x + \frac{y}{\sqrt{x^2 + y^2}} F^y \tag{5.12c}$$

$$F^\theta = \frac{x}{x^2 + y^2} F^x - \frac{y}{x^2 + y^2} F^y \tag{5.12d}$$

Note that in order for these equations to be well-formed, we cannot simply have r and θ take values in copies of $\mathbb{R}$. Rather, we require that r takes values in the (weakly) positive real numbers $R : = \{x \in \mathbb{R} : x \geq 0\}$ and that θ takes values in the interval $\Theta : = [0, 2\pi]$. Moreover, we identify any points where $r = 0$ with one another; and for any value of r, we identify the point $(r, 0)$ with

---

[60] Note that this theory is somewhat different from the usual expression of Newtonian mechanics in polar coordinates: that theory has F^θ on the right-hand side of (5.10b). (The expressions for translating between the two coordinate systems are correspondingly different, as well.) In brief, this is because the usual definition of 'angular force' is set up so as to compensate for the fact that the metric in polar coordinates does not have the form diag$(1, 1)$. I use the expressions here in order such that the transformation of force components is given by the standard formula (5.14).

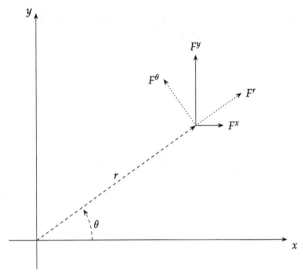

Figure 10 The relationship between the Cartesian and polar coordinate
systems.

$(r, 2\pi)$. In other words, we require that pairs (r, θ) take values in $R \times \Theta/_{\sim}$,
where $\sim$ is the equivalence relation

$$(r, \theta) \sim (r', \theta') \text{ iff } (r = r' = 0) \text{ or } (r = r', \theta = 0, \theta' = 2\pi) \qquad (5.13)$$

These conditions are, of course, consistent with the interpretations of r and θ
given above. There are no such restrictions on F^r and F^θ, so we suppose that
they take values in $\vec{R} \cong \mathbb{R}$ and $\vec{\Theta} \cong \mathbb{R}$, respectively.

The equations (5.11) can be thought of as providing a translation from (5.9)
to (5.10), in a sense analogous to that explored in Section 2. They show how
the simple predicates (i.e. the dependent variables) of (5.9) can be associated
with complex expressions of (5.10), in such a way that if we substitute the
dependent variables in (5.9) by the corresponding complex expressions, then
we obtain theorems of (5.10). In the same way, (5.12) provides a translation
from (5.10) to (5.9).

Moreover, recall that a translation from T_1 to T_2 induces a dual map from the
models of T_2 to the models of T_1. We find the same phenomenon here. Take as
given a solution to (5.10), i.e. a map of the form $(r(t), \theta(t))$. Then we can use
(5.11) to obtain a map of the form $(x(t), y(t))$ by setting $x(t) = r(t) \cos(\theta(t))$
and $y(t) = r(t) \sin(\theta(t))$. It is then not difficult to show that this map is a
solution to (5.9). Otherwise put, a solution of (5.10) consists of maps $\mathbb{T} \rightarrow$
$R \times \Theta/_{\sim}$ and $\mathbb{T} \rightarrow \vec{R} \times \vec{\Theta}$; (5.11) provides maps $R \times \Theta/_{\sim} \rightarrow X \times Y$ and
$\vec{R} \times \vec{\Theta} \rightarrow \vec{X} \times \vec{Y}$; and so, by composing these maps, we can obtain maps

$\mathbb{T} \to X \times Y$ and $\mathbb{T} \to \vec{X} \times \vec{Y}$, which turn out to constitute a solution to (5.9). Again, this holds good in the other direction: that is, (5.12) can be used to turn solutions to (5.9) into solutions to (5.10).

Finally, note that if we translate any expression of our theory using (5.11), and then translate it back using (5.12), then we get something which is equivalent modulo (5.9) to the original (indeed, we get something which is mathematically equivalent to the original); and the same when we translate using first (5.12) and then (5.11). This is, of course, the analogue of the condition (2.12) in the definition of intertranslatability (Definition 2.13). This indicates that we can think of the two theories (5.9) and (5.10) as intertranslatable, in a sense that is – at least – analogous to the formal notion discussed in Section 2.

As a final comment, note that in the above translations, we provided not only the coordinate transformations but also the appropriate transformations for the force terms. It is worth noting that these latter transformations are usually taken to be *entailed* by the coordinate transformations. The reason for this is that in specifying the theory, we should note that force is a directed, i.e. vectorial quantity. It follows that when we change coordinate systems, we also change how a given force quantity is decomposed into components. Specifically, a coordinate transformation from coordinates x^i to $\tilde{x}^i$ (with no assumption that the latter coordinates are Cartesian) implies a transformation of the force components from F^i to $\tilde{F}^i$, where

$$\tilde{F}^i = \sum_{j=1}^{3} \frac{\partial \tilde{x}^i}{\partial x^j} F^j \qquad (5.14)$$

It is not hard to show that this generates the appropriate results in the transformations given above.[61] Moving forward, we will suppose that force is indeed a vectorial quantity – and hence we will take the specification of a coordinate transformation to also fix the transformation of the force components.[62]

---

[61] As mentioned above (note 60), this would *not* be true if we used the standard expressions for doing Newtonian mechanics in polar coordinates. So the story is not quite as simple as the main text suggests!

[62] This is an example of a more general phenomenon. Many physical theories traffic in so-called *geometric objects*: objects that are described by components, where those components change in a fixed way in the transition from one coordinate system to another. For philosophical discussion of geometric objects, see Pitts (2010), Curiel (2019), Read (forthcoming), and references therein.

6 Symmetry

In this section, we turn our attention to the *symmetries* of Newtonian mechanics. The symmetries of a physical theory are often used as a guide to its interpretation, and in particular to the kind of structure that the theory should be interpreted as positing. The key to the interpretational role of symmetry is the following principle: that *symmetry-related solutions are physically equivalent*. Hence, symmetries stand as an especially important illustration of the intimate relationship between structure and equivalence. Note that until now, we have mostly discussed relationships of equivalence *between* theories; for symmetries, however, we must attend to the relationships of equivalence that might hold *within* a theory (specifically, that hold between the models of a theory). That said, symmetry will have implications for inter-theoretic relations of equivalence, as we shall see in subsequent sections.

6.1 Symmetries of Newtonian Mechanics

First, we must define what we mean by a 'symmetry'. The apparatus laid out in the previous section permits a pleasingly compact definition: a symmetry is a translation *between a theory and itself*. That is, we saw in the previous section that when we change coordinates, in general the syntactic form of our theory will change significantly: just compare (5.9) with (5.10). However, we find that for certain special transformations, the two theories have the same syntactic form. For the case of Newtonian mechanics, for example, consider the transformations from x^i to $\tilde{x}^i$, where

$$x^i = \sum_{j=1}^{3} R^i_j \tilde{x}^j + u^i t + a^i \tag{6.1}$$

for $a^i \in \mathbb{R}^3$, $u^i \in \mathbb{R}^3$, and R^i_j an orthogonal matrix (as we let i and j range from 1 to 3).[63] In the interests of a more compact notation, we will henceforth employ the *Einstein summation convention*: if an index is repeated, then summation over that index is implied. Thus, for example, we will take the expression $R^i_j \tilde{x}^j$ to be equivalent to $\sum_{j=1}^{3} R^i_j \tilde{x}^j$. It is straightforward to show that if we compose two transformations of the form (6.1), then we obtain another of the same form; and that for any transformation of this form, the inverse transformation is also of that form. Thus the transformations of the form (6.1) form a *group*.

---

[63] Recall that a matrix is *orthogonal* if its transpose is its inverse: thus to say that R^i_j is orthogonal is to say that $\sum_i R^i_j R^i_k = \delta_{jk}$, where δ_{jk} is the Kronecker delta.

Geometrically, we interpret the above transformations as comprising any combination of spatial translations (the a^i term), spatial rotations and reflections (the action of R^i_j), and Galilean boosts (the $u^i t$ term). The subgroup obtained by setting $u^i = 0$ (i.e. the group of spatial rotations, reflections, and translations) is known as the *Euclidean group*. The transformations (6.1) are a subgroup of the so-called *Galilean transformations*. The full group of Galilean transformations includes *temporal* translations and reflections, i.e. includes transformations of the form $t = \pm \tilde{t} + b$ (where $b \in \mathbb{R}$). It therefore includes transformations of the *independent variable t*, not just the dependent variables. Since our general discussion of coordinate transformations (in the previous section) was limited to transformations of dependent variables, and since it is transformations of that kind for which we best understand the analogy to the logical notions of definition and translation, we put aside transformations of independent variables. We will refer to the group of transformations (6.1) as the *isochronous Galilean group*.[64]

We now show that the isochronous Galilean transformations are symmetries of (5.1). First, in line with the discussion at the end of the previous section, the force term transforms in accordance with

$$F^i_n = R^i_j \tilde{F}^j_n \tag{6.2}$$

Applying these transformations to (5.1), we obtain

$$R^i_j m_n \frac{d^2 \tilde{x}^j_n}{dt^2} = R^i_j \tilde{F}^j_n \tag{6.3}$$

which is – once we've applied the inverse matrix to R^i_j on both sides – a notational variant of (5.1).

Note that in order for this procedure to work, we don't actually need R^i_j to be an orthogonal matrix: it will suffice that it be invertible. In this sense, the symmetry group of Newton's Second Law (alone) is *wider* than the Galilean group.[65] However, if we regard the force term not just as a placeholder but as some functional expression for the forces in terms of other physical quantities, then we can ask: are the new force-components $\tilde{F}^i_n$ (defined as per Eq. (6.2)), when expressed as functions of the new coordinates $\tilde{x}^i_n$, *of the same functional form* as the old force components F^i_n when those were expressed as functionsof

---

[64] This name is used by Lévy-Leblond (1971); I thank Bryan Roberts for drawing this work to my attention.

[65] See Wheeler (2007), Appendix 1.

the old coordinates x_n^i?[66] In other words, suppose we supplement Newton's
Second Law (5.1) by a force law of the schematic form

$$F_n^i = \Phi_n^i(t, x_p, v_p) \tag{6.4}$$

where $\Phi_n^i(t, x_p, v_p)$ is a functional expression featuring (in general) the time,
particle positions, and particle velocities – such as found in Eqs. (5.2), (5.3),
or (5.5). Then we can ask whether a given transformation of the coordinates –
and hence of the force-components – is a symmetry of this force law; that is,
whether substituting the expressions in (6.1) and (6.2) will enable us to derive

$$\tilde{F}_n^i = \Phi_n^i(t, \tilde{x}_p, \tilde{v}_p) \tag{6.5}$$

where $\tilde{v}_p^i := R_j^i v_p^j + u^i$.

And the answer to this question is that *if* the forces are independent of the
particle velocities, and if they depend only on inter-particle displacements, and
if they only depend on those either 'linear component-wise' or via distances –
then the symmetry group is the isochronous Galilean group.[67] More precisely,
the isochronous Galilean transformations will be symmetries if we suppose that
Φ_n^i takes the form

$$\Phi_n^i(t, x_p, v_p) = M^{km}{}_n(x_k^i - x_m^i) \tag{6.6}$$

where $M^{km}{}_n$ is an array of N^3 coefficients that depend only on time and on
the inter-particle distances (i.e. on expressions of the form $|x_n - x_p|$, defined
as in Eq. (5.4)). Thus, the force law (5.3) satisfies this condition, as does the
(trivial) force law (5.5); but the force law (5.2) does not.

As we discussed in §5.3, the transformation (6.1) will induce a map $\tilde{\mathbb{T}} \times \tilde{\mathbb{X}}$ to
$\mathbb{T} \times \mathbb{X}$; this will, in turn, induce a (bijective) mapping from solutions over the
latter space to solutions over the former space. However, if the transformation
is a symmetry, then the same differential equations will hold over both spaces,
and so we can interpret the transformation *actively* rather than *passively*: that is,
we can identify $\mathbb{X}$ with $\tilde{\mathbb{X}}$ and $\mathbb{T}$ with $\tilde{\mathbb{T}}$, and regard this map as a bijection from
the space of solutions over $\mathbb{T} \times \mathbb{X}$ to *itself*. This mapping will relate a given
solution to (5.1) to a solution which is (relative to it) translated, rotated, and
boosted. We now turn to the question of what the relationship is between these
solutions – and in particular, the idea that these solutions should be interpreted

---

[66] Compare Brown (2005), §3.2.

[67] If the forces are furthermore independent of time, then the symmetry group will be the full
Galilei group. The fact that the symmetry group depends on the nature of the force laws – in
particular, on whether they are velocity-independent or not – is discussed in Brown (2005), §3.2,
and Barbour (1989).

as equivalent, in the sense that they describe the same physical events in a (merely) mathematically distinct way.

6.2 Symmetry and Equivalence

The idea that symmetries are physical equivalences has a long history, especially in the context of Newtonian mechanics. Indeed, it goes back (at least) to the famous correspondence of Leibniz and Clarke: "To say that God can cause the whole universe to move forward in a right line, or in any other line, without making otherwise any alteration in it; is another chimerical supposition. For, two states indiscernible from each other, are the same state; and consequently, 'tis a change without any change."[68] This quotation also points towards one of the key ideas underpinning this interpretational move, at least in the current literature: the idea that Galilean symmetries hold between models that are indiscernible from one another, or (as we would say now) that they are *empirically equivalent*.[69] The argument for this goes, roughly, as follows:

P1 To say that two models are empirically discernible is to say that some quantity could be measured to have different values in the two models.

P2 To measure a physical quantity is to set up a dynamical process which reliably and systematically correlates the value of that quantity with some independent quantity belonging to the measuring device.

P3 Symmetries commute with the dynamics: applying a symmetry transformation and letting a system evolve delivers the same result as letting the system evolve and then applying the symmetry transformation.

P4 The quantities in which a measuring device can record results, and the appropriate operating conditions for a measuring device, are invariant under symmetry transformations.

C1 So if a measuring device ends up in a certain state when the symmetry is not applied, then it will end up in the same state when the symmetry is applied.

C2 Hence, there is no way of reliably correlating a symmetry-variant quantity with the end state of the measuring device.

P1 and P2 are plausible definitions of the notions of 'empirically discernible' and 'measurement'. In the case of Newtonian mechanics, P3 is easy to verify for the case of the *Euclidean* transformations. For example, suppose that we rotate a system in space, and then let it evolve. In the end, the result is the same

---

[68] Alexander (1956), p. 38.
[69] Exactly what role empirical equivalence plays in Leibniz's own argument(s) for this conclusion is a rather more vexed question, and not one that we will go into here.

as what we would have got if we had let the system evolve and then rotated it at the end. The same goes, reasonably clearly, for spatial translations.

For boosts, the argument is a little trickier: strictly speaking, boosts do *not* commute with the dynamics, since a boosted system will evolve into a system that is spatially translated relative to what we would have obtained by first evolving and then boosting. However, since spatial translations are themselves a symmetry, we can use a bootstrapping procedure: if the argument works for the Euclidean subgroup, then we can run a similar argument for the whole synchronous Galilean group by replacing P3 with

P3* Applying a symmetry transformation and letting a system evolve delivers the same result, within physical equivalence, as letting the system evolve then applying the symmetry transformation.

It is natural to think that the premise of P3 (or P3*) is not somehow specific to the case of Newtonian mechanics: it should seem intuitively plausible that this is a general feature of symmetry transformations. Showing this is not entirely straightforward, primarily because a rather high degree of abstraction is required; nevertheless, Wallace (n.d.-b) gives the relevant argument. Thus, although our remarks in this Element will be confined to the particular case of Newtonian mechanics, one can reasonably anticipate that they should generalise to symmetries more generally.

In other words, P3 (or P3*) asserts the *autonomy* of the symmetry-invariant quantities from the symmetry-variant quantities. If we know a system's state to within a symmetry transformation at one time, then we can predict its state to within a symmetry transformation at a later time. Hence, changing symmetry-variant quantities has no implications for the evolution of the symmetry-invariant quantities. It is perhaps worth noting that this does not hold in the other direction: if we alter symmetry-invariant quantities, then in general – and insofar as the question is well-posed – the symmetry-variant quantities will evolve differently from how they would have otherwise. For example, if we take a pair of particles in a stable orbit and move particle 2 away from particle 1 (hence increasing their relative distance), then the position of particle 1 will evolve differently compared to how it would have done so otherwise.

Finally, we turn to premise P4. The premises P1, P2, and P3 (or P3*) suffice to show that one cannot use the invariant degrees of freedom to measure the symmetry-variant degrees of freedom (and hence that symmetry-related solutions are empirically equivalent). P4 asserts that one cannot use the symmetry-*variant* degrees of freedom to do so, either. For example, the facts about an object's absolute position over time certainly encode facts about its absolute velocity. So suppose that someone proposed using absolute position as a means of measuring absolute velocity. Alternatively, suppose that someone provided us with a device that measures an object's velocity relative to itself, and then claimed that this device measures absolute velocity – but that the device only functions properly when it is itself at absolute rest. P4 rests on the intuitively plausible idea that there's something defective about these proposals; can we say anything enlightening about what that something is?[70]

Broadly speaking, one can discern three proposed answers to this question in the literature. One answer points to the fact that absolute position and velocity are *unobservable*, in the sense that we as humans cannot perceive them directly; the above argument is then understood as showing that they cannot be indirectly detected, either. This answer then (typically) goes on to conjecture that the definition of symmetry should include the requirement that symmetry-related models are (in some appropriate sense) observationally equivalent. For examples of this answer, see Dasgupta (2016) and Ismael and van Fraassen (2003).

A second answer points toward considerations from philosophy of language. The idea here is that even if we were able to detect symmetry-variant quantities by recording the result in other symmetry-variant quantities, the knowledge that would thereby be gained would exhibit a peculiar form of *untransmissibility* or *unencodability*. We cannot (for example) encode the 'result' of this detection by such familiar means as writing it down, or weaving it into a tapestry, or sending it via email; it would therefore violate a principle that any reliably manipulable physical process can be used as a channel for communicating knowledge. Roberts (2008) outlines a concern of this kind.

Finally, Wallace (n.d.-b) has argued that the problem with a 'measurement' of this kind is that the quantity being measured and the quantity being used to encode the measurement result are insufficiently independent of one another. To motivate this answer, consider the proposal that we use an object's absolute velocity as a measure of its own absolute velocity: certainly, these two quantities are guaranteed to covary with one another, but it seems wrong to think of this as a *measurement*. Paraphrasing somewhat, Wallace then argues that when we take an appropriately abstract dynamical perspective, we end up recognising the symmetry-variant data as constituting a single quantity. It will then follow that the proposals above are defective for the same reason.

---

[70] Not all authors agree that proposals along these lines are defective, however: see Middleton and Ramírez (2021) for a defence of the claim that absolute velocity *is* measurable in Newtonian mechanics (and Jacobs (forthcoming) for a response).

There is not the space here to defend any of these answers in detail, or to discuss further nuances.[71] However, we will take it that one of these answers can be made to work; or at least, that there is clearly something defective about the proposal to record measurements of symmetry-variant data in other symmetry-variant data. Helping ourselves to that assumption, we conclude (on the basis of the autonomy of the symmetry-invariant data) that no non-defective measurement of symmetry-variant quantities is possible after all. Together with plausible Occamist norms about not having undetectable quantities in one's physics, this motivates the interpretation of symmetry-related models as physically equivalent; or in other words, the interpretation of symmetry-variant quantities as 'surplus structure'. In the next section, we examine the consequences of adopting such an interpretation for our account of symmetry and equivalence in Newtonian mechanics.

7 Galilean Spacetime

So, suppose we make the assumption that symmetry-related states of affairs should be regarded as physically equivalent. The natural next step is to find some way of presenting our theory so that the symmetry-related states of affairs are more manifestly equivalent; that is, to find a version of the theory such that symmetry-related models are mathematically equivalent.[72] For us, that will mean setting the theory not on $\mathbb{T} \times \mathbb{X}$ (which is, recall, isomorphic to $\mathbb{R}^4$), but rather on the substructure of $\mathbb{T} \times \mathbb{X}$ that is invariant under the action of the isochronous Galilean group.

---

[71] One very important such nuance is that the discussion here only concerns the case where we seek to record the result of measuring some quantity of the system in other quantities of that same system; thus we have neglected any discussion of how things stand when we think about relationships between *subsystems*. Yet such cases are crucial to a proper understanding of the empirical significance of symmetries: see Kosso (2000), Brading and Brown (2004), Healey (2009), Greaves and Wallace (2014), Wallace (n.d.-a), and references therein.

[72] Indeed, on some analyses of symmetry, it is an error to – as we have done here – interpret symmetries as relating physically equivalent states of affairs before having such a redundancy-eliminating alternative to hand. In the terminology of Møller-Nielsen (2017), the viewpoint taken here (where one interprets symmetries as physical equivalences before reformulating the theory) is referred to as the *interpretationalist* approach; the alternative (where a symmetry may only be interpreted as a physical equivalence once such a reformulation has been found) is referred to as the *motivationalist* approach, since symmetries merely provide motivation for seeking an appropriate reformulation, not warrant for such an interpretation. For defences of the motivationalist approach, see Møller-Nielsen (2017), Read and Møller-Nielsen (2020); for the interpretationalist approach, see Saunders (2003).

7.1 Euclidean Invariance

We start by considering the action of the Euclidean group on $\mathbb{X}$, and ask what substructure of $\mathbb{X}$ is invariant under this group action. It is best to begin with the action of the (three-dimensional) orthogonal group $O(3)$, i.e. the group of all rotations and reflections. So let R^i_j be an orthogonal matrix, and consider the mapping from $\mathbb{X}$ to itself given by

$$x^i \mapsto R^i_j x^j \tag{7.1}$$

We start by observing that the *vector-space* structure of $\mathbb{X}$ is preserved, since the mapping (7.1) is a linear map; moreover, we observe that since R^i_j is an orthogonal matrix, the Euclidean inner product on $\mathbb{X}$ is preserved. In other words, rotations and reflections preserve not only the linear structure of $\mathbb{X}$, but also the distance from any point to the origin.[73] Thus the structure of $\mathbb{X}$ invariant under rotations and reflections includes, at least, the structure of a Euclidean vector space. Furthermore, it turns out that the structure of a Euclidean vector space *exhausts* the invariant structure of $\mathbb{X}$, in the following sense: the only automorphisms of a Euclidean vector space are the rotations and reflections. Thus replacing $\mathbb{X}$ with its $O(3)$-invariant substructure means replacing it with a Euclidean vector space, which we shall denote $\mathfrak{X}$.

However, we don't want the theory to be invariant only under rotations and reflections: it should also be invariant under translations. Therefore, we need to pick out the substructure of $\mathfrak{X}$ which is invariant under translations.[74] As is well-known, the translation-invariant substructure of a vector space is an *affine* space; and the translation-invariant substructure of an inner-product space is a *metric* affine space. So the Euclidean-invariant substructure of $\mathbb{X}$ is a three-dimensional Euclidean affine space. We denote this affine space by $\mathcal{X}$.

This lets us state our theory in 'Euclidean-invariant' terms. Rather than having our particles' locations take values in $\mathbb{X} \cong \mathbb{R}^3$, let us instead have them take values in affine Euclidean space $\mathcal{X}$; we will use the (non-indexed) variable x_n for the location of the nth particle. Furthermore, in line with our recognition of force as a vectorial quantity, let us have the forces take values in $\mathfrak{X}$. We replace the triple of variables F^i_n with the $\mathfrak{X}$-valued variable $\vec{F}_n$.

We can now write down the following new version of (5.1):

$$m_n \frac{d^2 x_n}{dt^2} = \vec{F}_n \tag{7.2}$$

---

[73] This gloss – that preservation of the inner product is equivalent to preservation of the norm – exploits the fact that Euclidean inner products and Euclidean norms are interdefinable.

[74] The vector space $\mathfrak{X}$, if regarded as a candidate for physical space, is referred to in the literature as *Aristotelian space*.

This equation is well-formed: given an $\mathcal{X}$-valued curve parameterised by $\mathbb{T}$, its derivative is an $\mathfrak{X}$-valued curve parameterised by $\mathbb{T}$; and the derivative of *that* curve is another $\mathfrak{X}$-valued curve parameterised by $\mathbb{T}$. Thus it makes sense to demand that (7.2) holds at all times in $\mathbb{T}$.

7.2 Galilean Invariance

Now, we consider boosts. First, we should observe that whereas the Euclidean group has an action on space alone, boosts do not: because the action of a boost is parameterised by t, we need to consider it as an action on *spacetime*. That is, let us define *horological Newtonian spacetime* as the product space $\mathbb{T} \times \mathcal{X}$, and denote it $\mathcal{N}_0$.[75] A boost acts on this structure as follows: given any $(t, x) \in \mathbb{T} \times \mathcal{X}$, a boost along $\vec{u} \in \mathfrak{X}$ acts according to

$$t \mapsto t \tag{7.3}$$

$$x \mapsto x + \vec{u}t \tag{7.4}$$

As has often been observed, Newtonian spacetime structure is not invariant under boosts. To see this, note that there is a well-defined relation between points of $\mathcal{N}_0$ of *corresponding to the same spatial point*: this holds between any pair of spacetime points of the form (t, x) and (t', x).[76] However, this relation is not preserved under the action of a boost, since it will map such a pair of spacetime points to the pair of spacetime points $(t, x + \vec{u}t)$ and $(t', x + \vec{u}t')$ – i.e. a pair which, in general, do not correspond to the same spatial point.

We therefore seek the invariant substructure of $\mathcal{N}_0$. We will call this substructure *horological Galilean spacetime*, and define it as follows:[77]

Definition 7.1 A *horological Galilean spacetime* is a four-dimensional affine space $\mathcal{G}_0$, whose associated vector space $\mathfrak{G}$ contains $\mathfrak{X}$ as a subspace, and whose quotient space $\mathcal{G}_0 \big/ \mathfrak{X}$ is isomorphic to $\mathbb{T}$.

---

[75] Newtonian spacetime was introduced in Stein (1967). The structure here differs from Newtonian spacetime, as defined by Stein, in that it has an 'absolute clock' (hence the term 'horological'): that is, a temporal origin and orientation. (Note that Newtonian spacetime as defined by, for instance, Friedman (1983) or Earman (1989) has a temporal orientation, although no temporal origin. See Malament (2012), p. 251.)

[76] More formally, this relation is the equivalence relation whose equivalence classes are the preimages of the projection map $\mathcal{N}_0 \to \mathcal{X}$, for all points of $\mathcal{X}$.

[77] What we now call Galilean or neo-Newtonian spacetime is also discussed in Stein (1967); see also Saunders (2013). As with Newtonian spacetime, the structure here differs from 'normal' Galilean spacetime in having a temporal origin and orientation.

A fuller definition of $\mathcal{G}_0$ is therefore as a set equipped with a free, transitive action of a four-dimensional vector space $\mathfrak{G}$, and furthermore with both a privileged embedding $\mathcal{X} \to \mathfrak{G}$ and a privileged affine bijection $\mathcal{G}_0/\mathcal{X} \to \mathbb{T}$. If we examine the automorphisms of this structure, then we find that they are – as desired – precisely the isochronous Galilean transformations.

We will say that a Galilean vector $\vec{\xi} \in \mathfrak{G}$ is *purely spatial* if $\vec{\xi} \in \mathcal{X}$; it is worth stressing that there is no analogous notion of a Galilean vector's being 'purely temporal'. The presence of $\mathcal{X}$ as a subspace of $\mathfrak{G}$ means that $\mathcal{G}_0$ is foliated into three-dimensional subspaces, each isomorphic to $\mathcal{X}$ – that is, where the elements of each three-dimensional subspace are related by purely spatial vectors. The fact that the quotient space is isomorphic to $\mathbb{T}$ (which is, remember, just a copy of $\mathbb{R}$) means that each spacetime point of $\mathcal{G}_0$ is labelled by some value of time: that is, we have a *clock function* $\chi : \mathcal{G}_0 \to \mathbb{T}$. Since this is obtained by composing the quotient map with the isomorphism to $\mathbb{T}$, spacetime points in the same three-dimensional subspace (i.e. spacetime points related by purely spatial vectors) are labelled by the same value of time. In other words, the three-dimensional subspaces represent simultaneity hypersurfaces. We also use the clock function to define the *temporal length* of Galilean vectors: given a Galilean vector $\vec{\xi}$, its temporal length is the difference in clock values for any pair of points in $\mathcal{G}_0$ separated by $\vec{\xi}$. (It is straightforward to show that this is independent of what pair of points is chosen.)

The key difference from Newtonian spacetime, then, is that there is no 'persistence of space over time': since there is no notion of a vector being 'purely temporal', we cannot say of two points in $\mathcal{G}_0$ that they differ by a purely temporal vector, and hence correspond to the same point of space at two different times. (By contrast, since we do have a notion of purely spatial vectors, we can say of two points of $\mathcal{G}_0$ that they differ by such a vector and hence correspond to two different points of space at the same time; this is precisely the relation that foliates $\mathcal{G}_0$.)

Finally, then, we wish to state our theory of Newtonian mechanics in terms of these structures. To do so, we will take a specification of the particle positions over time to consist of N smooth curves $\gamma_n : \mathbb{T} \to \mathcal{G}_0$, all of which are such that for any $t \in \mathbb{T}$, $\chi(\gamma_n(t)) = t$.[78] It follows that the derivative $d\gamma_n/dt$ is (at any time) a Galilean four-vector whose temporal length is 1; and hence that the second derivative $d^2\gamma_n/dt^2$ is (again, at any time) a purely spatial Galilean vector. So, letting forces take values in $\mathcal{X} \subseteq \mathfrak{G}$, our final formulation of

---

[78] For those familiar with fibre bundles: if we think of $\mathcal{G}_0$ as a fibre bundle over $\mathbb{T}$ (with standard fibre $\mathcal{X}$ and bundle projection χ), then this amounts to requiring that each trajectory be a section of the bundle.

Newtonian mechanics consists of the equation

$$m_n \frac{d^2 \gamma_n}{dt^2} = \vec{F}_n \tag{7.5}$$

The upshot of all this is that if two solutions $(\gamma_n, \vec{F}_n)$ and $(\gamma'_n, \vec{F}'_n)$ are related by an isochronous Galilean transformation, then they are *isomorphic* to one another. More precisely, there is an isomorphism $g : \mathcal{G}_0 \to \mathcal{G}_0$, inducing an isomorphism $\hat{g} : \mathfrak{G} \to \mathfrak{G}$, such that for all $t \in \mathbb{T}$, $g(\gamma_n(t)) = \gamma'_n(t)$ and $\hat{g}(\vec{F}_n(t)) = \vec{F}'_n(t)$; that is, such that the following diagrams commute:

$$\begin{array}{ccc}
\mathbb{T} \xrightarrow{\gamma_n} \mathcal{G}_0 & \qquad & \mathbb{T} \xrightarrow{\vec{F}_n} \mathfrak{G} \\
\searrow{\scriptstyle \gamma'_n} \quad \downarrow{\scriptstyle g} & & \searrow{\scriptstyle \vec{F}'_n} \quad \downarrow{\scriptstyle \hat{g}} \\
\mathcal{G}_0 & & \mathfrak{G}
\end{array} \tag{7.6}$$

As a result, $(\gamma_n, \vec{F}_n)$ and $(\gamma'_n, \vec{F}'_n)$ are isomorphic. So, as desired, we have reformulated our theory in such a way that physical equivalence corresponds to mathematical isomorphism.

There is a great deal of debate in the literature about whether this kind of structural equivalence is enough, or whether something stricter is required – such as a formulation of the theory in which symmetry-related models are *identical* (not just isomorphic). For the most part, this debate takes it as read that structurally equivalent models agree on the distribution of qualitative properties, and therefore concerns the acceptability of arguing on purely philosophical grounds (i.e. without further mathematical work) that there are no non-qualitative differences between possible worlds. However, since this debate (over so-called 'sophisticated substantivalism') mostly concerns metaphysical issues that are orthogonal to our main interests in this work, we leave it aside.[79]

7.3 Symmetry and Structure

Looking back at the above, we see that we have considered three structures for representing spacetime: the 'coordinate spacetime' $\mathbb{T} \times \mathbb{X} \cong \mathbb{R}^4$, horological Newtonian spacetime $\mathcal{N}_0 = \mathbb{T} \times \mathcal{X}$, and horological Galilean spacetime $\mathcal{G}_0$. Each of these spacetime structures contains, in some intuitively clear sense, strictly less structure than the one before it. One way to try to cash this out is in terms of definability: anything which is definable in $\mathcal{G}_0$ is definable in $\mathcal{N}_0$, and anything definable in $\mathcal{N}_0$ is definable in $\mathbb{T} \times \mathbb{X}$. Even this is not fully precise,

---

[79] For discussion of this issue, see Pooley (2006) and references therein.

absent a clarification of the language in which we are allowing definitions, but even so it is a helpful way to think about what is going on.

In Section 1, we saw that there was a close link between definability and invariance. This suggests that we should also compare the automorphism groups of the different structures. The automorphism group of $\mathbb{T} \times \mathbb{X}$ is the trivial group, consisting of just the identity mapping – $\mathbb{T} \times \mathbb{X}$ is, as we say, a 'rigid' structure (one possessing no non-trivial automorphisms). The automorphism group of $\mathcal{N}_0$ is the Euclidean group; and the automorphism group of $\mathcal{G}_0$ is the isochronous Galilean group. Each of these groups is a subgroup of the next. Thus, as the automorphism group grows, the 'amount of structure' shrinks.[80]

Barrett (2015b) formulates this as the following principle, which he calls SYM*:

> A mathematical object X has more structure than a mathematical object Y if $\text{Aut}(X) \subsetneq \text{Aut}(Y)$.[81]

As Barrett notes, and as Wilhelm (2021) expands upon, this criterion is only really appropriately applied in cases where X and Y share an underlying set: otherwise, the automorphism groups will trivially not be included in one another. Nevertheless, so long as that assumption can be made in a reasonably harmless way, it proves to be a helpful organising principle for classifying different spacetimes according to their automorphism groups.[82]

Indeed, we can consider using invariance groups as a way of specifying a structure (rather than specifying a structure in some other fashion, and then examining its invariances). That is, rather than the 'intrinsic' definition of horological Galilean spacetime that was given in Definition 7.1, we could define it by the condition that it consists of the substructure of $\mathbb{R}^4$ invariant under the isochronous Galilean group. Wallace (2019) refers to this as the *structured-space* approach to defining spacetime structures (and gives a detailed defence of its usefulness and conceptual cogency).

The structured-space approach can be developed using category-theoretic tools. Consider the following categories of models (Table 1):

---

[80] This idea has come up in debates on the structure of classical mechanics: see North (2009), Swanson and Halvorson (n.d.), Curiel (2014), and Barrett (2015a).

[81] Barrett (2015a), p. 38.

[82] In practice, this means that it is most helpful for comparing different flat spacetimes that are all homeomorphic to $\mathbb{R}^4$.

Table 1 Categories of models for Newtonian mechanics.

Category	Objects	Morphisms
Newt_1	Solutions to (5.1)	Only identity morphisms
Newt_2	Solutions to (7.5)	Isomorphisms of solutions, as in (7.6)
Newt_3	Solutions to (5.1)	Isochronous Galilean transformations of solutions, as in (6.1)

Thus the objects of Newt_1 and Newt_3 are models of Newtonian mechanics set on coordinate spacetime, whereas those of Newt_2 are models of Newtonian mechanics set on horological Galilean spacetime. In both Newt_1 and Newt_2, the arrows are isomorphisms of the explicitly posited structure (recall that coordinate spacetime is rigid, and so has no non-trivial such isomorphisms). In Newt_3, the arrows are different to those we would 'expect', given the spacetime structure that has been explicitly introduced.

We then have the following result:

Proposition 7.2 The categories Newt_2 and Newt_3 are equivalent.

Proof By regarding $\mathcal{G}_0$ as a substructure of $\mathbb{T} \times \mathbb{X}$, we can associate every solution $(x_n^i(t), F_n^i(t))$ of (5.1) with a solution $(\gamma_n, \vec{F}_n)$ of (7.5). Moreover, given two solutions to (5.1) related by an isochronous Galilean transformation, there will be an isomorphism g of $\mathcal{G}_0$ relating the corresponding solutions to (7.5). So, let $G : \text{Newt}_3 \to \text{Newt}_2$ be defined as taking solutions of (5.1) to the corresponding solution of (7.5), and isochronous Galilean transformations to the corresponding isomorphisms of $\mathcal{G}_0$. Showing that G is a functor, and that it is full, faithful, and surjective, is left as an exercise.

Since the proof of equivalence involves the explicit construction of a functor from Newt_3 to Newt_2, then we can even regard this equivalence as induced by a translation: in effect, the translation we obtain by noting that the structures of $\mathcal{G}_0$ can be defined in terms of $\mathbb{T} \times \mathbb{X}$.[83] It is not entirely clear whether they are categorically equivalent to Newt_1 – but it at least seems plausible to conjecture that they are not categorically equivalent by such a 'translational' functor.[84]

These observations motivate the following interpretation of the above categories. The objects of the category are defined or described using certain

---

[83] More carefully, one would expect that Newt_2 and Newt_3 could be shown to be definably categorically equivalent in the sense of Hudetz (2019).

[84] Compare Hudetz (2019), Proposition 5.

mathematical structures: affine spaces, coordinates, or whatever. The arrows of the category then indicate which parts of these structures are to be 'taken seriously', and which are to be regarded as surplus structure – scaffolding to be discarded, as it were. Thus, $Newt_1$ and $Newt_2$ describe theories that lack such surplus structures, since the arrows are exactly those which are native to the structures on the objects. In $Newt_3$, however, although coordinates were used to characterise the objects, the arrows tell us that these coordinates are mere surplus structures.[85] On this interpretation, then, we can think of $Newt_3$ as Newtonian mechanics set on Galilean spacetime – but where Galilean spacetime has been characterised using a structured-space approach rather than a more intrinsic approach. The fact that it is (translationally) categorically equivalent to $Newt_2$ is interpreted as reflecting the fact that the structural commitments of these two theories are in fact the same, the difference in how they characterise those commitments notwithstanding.

There is plenty more to be said about these issues, at both the technical and conceptual level. In a little volume such as this, however, there is no space to do so; we turn instead to wrapping up and reflecting on what we've learned.

8 Conclusion

8.1 Equivalence and Interpretation

Thus concludes our tour of how notions of structure and equivalence play out in various contexts. In this final section, I want to take a bit of a step back, and look at some of the conceptual significance of what we've done here. In particular, there is a concern about the kind of approach that has been taken here, where we have focused on formal and mathematical considerations: namely, that formal criteria of equivalence are a mere change of subject. Surely – so the thought goes – we care about whether theories are *actually* equivalent to one another, i.e. whether they have the same semantic content; and surely that can't be determined just on the basis of comparing formalisms?

Sklar (1982) puts the point as follows. After noting that for realists, empirical equivalence is not going to be sufficient for theoretical equivalence, he notes that many realists are attracted to the idea that we should also require that the two theories exhibit some appropriate kind of 'structural interrelationship'. But, he continues, this interrelationship

> cannot be a purely formal notion. It cannot be, that is, an interrelationship which can be determined to hold solely on the basis of the logical form of the theories in question. Why not? We will consider the strongest such possible

---

[85] A significantly more sophisticated discussion of this point is in Hudetz (2019), §4.3.

formal interrelationship one can imagine. Let us suppose that the theories are term by term 'inter-translatable', that is, that each can be obtained from the other merely by a substitution of terms of one theory for terms of the other. Would that be enough to show the theories equivalent?

Surely not. Let the two theories be 'All lions have stripes', and 'All tigers have stripes', with all the words in both theories taking on their usual meanings. The theories are inter-translatable in the purely formal sense. They are exactly alike in logical form and one can be obtained from the other by a simple term for term substitution. But they are most assuredly not equivalent.[86]

Sklar's point is well-taken: evidently, the existence of a formal equivalence cannot be sufficient (by itself) for sameness of semantic content. To explore this in more detail, and to make stronger the connection to problems in philosophy of physics, let us return to the pair of theories discussed in Section 5: the two formulations (5.9) and (5.10) of two-dimensional Newtonian mechanics in (respectively) Cartesian and polar coordinates. As usually understood, this example is a paradigm case of theoretical equivalence. The theories (5.9) and (5.10) are typically taken to describe the same physics, just with different choices of how to label the points of the plane: namely, by x-distance from the origin and y-distance from the origin, or by radial distance from the origin and subtended angle. The theories do indeed look very different, but – so we usually imagine – that indicates very little about the semantic content of what those theories express.

However, a little reflection indicates that this judgment of equivalence is not as automatic as it might seem. In particular, consider the following physical system. It takes place on a rather odd two-dimensional geometry, illustrated in Figure 11: a cylinder truncated perpendicular to its length, of unit radius, such that all the points at the closed end of the cylinder have been identified with one another. In other words, this geometry is the quotient space $R \times \Theta/_\sim$ that was described in Section 5.

Now consider a single particle moving on the surface of the cylinder. Using r as the coordinate along the length of the cylinder and θ as the angular coordinate

---

[86] Sklar (1982), p. 93. It is perhaps worth noting that the criterion Sklar describes is not the condition of intertranslatability as described in Section 2: depending on how we interpret Sklar's words, it is either what we called mutual translatability, or (perhaps) a condition of mutual *conservative* translatability (a conservative translation being a translation $\tau : T_1 \rightarrow T_2$ such that if $T_2 \vdash \tau\phi$, then $T_1 \vdash \phi$ (Halvorson, 2019)). Mutual conservative translatability, although stronger than mutual translatability, is nevertheless weaker than intertranslatability (Barrett and Halvorson, n.d.). (See also the comparison of mutual faithful interpretability to biinterpretability and definitional equivalence in Button and Walsh (2018), §5.5.) Of course, this doesn't affect Sklar's point, since the example in question is intertranslatable in our, stronger sense.

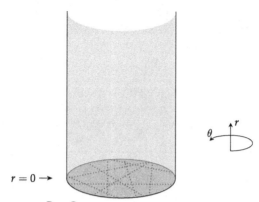

$r = 0 \rightarrow$

Figure 11 The space $R \times \Theta / {\sim}$: the dotted lines illustrate the identity relation that holds between all points at r = 0.

around the cylinder, suppose that the laws governing its motion are those given in Eq. (5.10). For example, for a free particle, one can show that the relationship between r and θ for generic solutions to (5.10) is

$$r = \frac{c}{a \cos \theta + b \sin \theta} \tag{8.1}$$

for $a, b, c \in \mathbb{R}$. An example is illustrated in Fig. 12: the particle descends almost vertically for large r; then for small r it swerves around to the other side of the cylinder and begins ascending again, once more approaching a near-vertical trajectory.[87]

Prima facie, this looks like a very different physics to the physics which (5.9) describes as holding on the plane. In particular, imagine a three-dimensional world, in which there exists both a plane on which (5.9) holds, and a half-cylinder on which (5.10) holds. It seems clearly incorrect to say that particles on the plane and particles on the half-cylinder exhibit the same behaviour. For example, as we have just discussed, free particles on the cylinder do not move in straight lines: they swerve and curve as they approach the bottom of the cylinder.

It is natural to now say something like the following: like 'All lions have stripes' and 'All tigers have stripes', what this demonstrates is that the formal intertranslatability of (5.9) and (5.10) can only, at best, be part of the story when it comes to the question of whether these two theories are equivalent; we

---

[87] This is true only for 'generic' solutions because there is also the special case where the particle begins with pure vertical motion, i.e. motion purely in the r-direction. In this case, the particle descends vertically until it reaches $r = 0$, then ascends vertically on the opposite side of the cylinder. (Note that this is still a continuous trajectory, since all points of $r = 0$ have been identified with one another.)

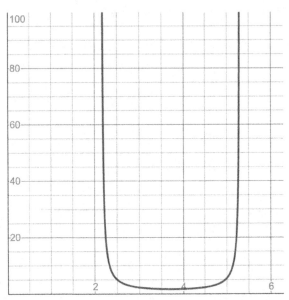

Figure 12 The trajectory of a free particle in the half-cylinder: r is on the vertical axis, θ is on the horizontal axis. (Figure created using the Desmos graphing calculator, available at https://www.desmos.com/calculator.)

need, in addition, to say something about the *interpretation* of the formalism. In this case, we first considered an interpretation according to which r represented the radial distance from the origin and θ the subtended angle; we then considered a different interpretation according to which r represented the vertical cylindrical distance and θ the angular distance. Indeed, we could even reinterpret the theory (5.9) so that it describes physics on the half-cylinder rather than the plane: (5.11) indicates how any point on the half-cylinder can be described by a pair of coordinates (x, y), and in this coordinate system the half-cylinder's physics will be expressed by (5.9). So (at least) two interpretations of each formalism are available, and with different interpretations come, naturally, different relations of equivalence. Indeed, on this line of thought, the formal intertranslatability starts to look like a sideshow: two formalisms are equivalent if they are assigned the same interpretation, and inequivalent if they are assigned different interpretations.[88]

---

[88] See Coffey (2014) or Teitel (2021) for a fuller version of this line of argument; see also Maudlin (2018) for a general account of how mathematical theories must be accompanied by a 'commentary' in order to fix their physical interpretation.

8.2 Equivalence as Interpretation

However, when we start to examine this idea of 'supplying' an interpretation, we begin running into some more difficult questions. Presumably, the interpretation itself must be specified in some appropriate language. So we then must confront the question: why is *that* language in any better shape than the language with which we began? What fixes the interpretation of (the linguistic statement of) the interpretation? In particular, consider again the way in which an 'embedding' of the two geometries into a three-dimensional geometry was used to motivate the idea that they are distinct. The problem is that these are not the only possible ways of mapping our two-dimensional geometries into a three-dimensional space. In particular, there is (of course!) a way of mapping the unit half-cylinder to the x-y-plane in $\mathbb{R}^3$: a point (r, θ) on the half-cylinder (r the vertical distance, θ the angular distance) is mapped to the point $(r \cos \theta, r \sin \theta)$. Conversely, there is also a way of mapping the plane to the half-cylinder (in $\mathbb{R}^3$). So we cannot use these considerations to show that the plane and the half-cylinder are somehow 'intrinsically' different interpretations: whether they seem different or not depends on what mappings to $\mathbb{R}^3$ are under consideration.[89]

Clearly, an infinite regress threatens. Teitel (2021) notes this problem: after arguing that 'natural language glosses' are an indispensable part of how theories in physics are endowed with semantic content, he continues

> Of course these brief remarks are only the beginning of a complete story about how mathematical physics works: we still face the question of how some of these antecedently understood concepts come to have content in the first place, whether our concept of space, time, object, and so on. However, this is just the familiar and perennial problem of metasemantics, which is everyone's problem, and the subject of considerable ongoing investigation. Given that mathematical physics works, and natural language glosses involving these concepts play an important role in its operation, the problem must have some solution.[90]

What this neglects, though, is the possibility that formal criteria of equivalence might be relevant to the project of developing an appropriate metasemantic theory. In particular, there must be some constraints on what interpretation can be assigned to a given formalism. But in assigning a particular interpretation to a formalism, we are asserting that the interpretation and the formalism

---

[89] This indicates that these questions are closely connected to problems about the conventionality of geometry.

[90] Teitel (2021), pp. 4146–4147.

are equivalent! So the constraints on acceptable interpretation will surely mirror the constraints on equivalence. Indeed, from this perspective, it seems that assertions about the interpretation of a formalism, far from being a precondition to assertions about equivalence, are in fact just a special case of assertions about equivalence. When we offer Galilean spacetime, as defined in Definition 7.1, as the best interpretation of the spacetime structure for Newtonian mechanics in coordinates (5.1), what we are really doing is asserting that (5.1) should be regarded as equivalent to the theory (7.5) of Newtonian mechanics on Galilean spacetime. Such an assertion will only be legitimate if we can – in Sklar's terminology – find an appropriate way of relating the structures of the two theories to one another. I take it that one of the key insights of recent work on formal notions of equivalence has been to recognise that this need not be a relationship that is anything like as strong as 'structural isomorphism': in particular, we saw in Section 7 how categorical notions of equivalence seem well-suited to expressing relations of equivalence between formalisms with different amounts of nominal or apparent structure. Nor is that fact specific to the example of Newtonian mechanics, as the growing literature on categorical equivalence indicates.[91]

Once again, though, this is not to say that these formal constraints are the only constraints on assertions of equivalence. If we cannot appeal to meanings as the further constraint, though, then how do we answer Sklar's challenge? I want to suggest that the key to doing so was, in fact, already anticipated in Sklar's discussion: we have not just the condition of formal equivalence, but also the condition of *empirical* equivalence. However, the advocate of formal criteria should not regard this as a mere conjunction of conditions: that theories should be formally equivalent, and then also empirically equivalent (in whatever preferred sense). Rather, they should be empirically equivalent *via the chosen formal equivalence*: the formal equivalence should, as it were, 'commute with the empirical predictions'.[92]

Thus the reason why our theories about lions and tigers are distinct is because under the proposed translation, empirical content fails to be preserved – lions and tigers being associated with distinct empirical consequences. Similarly, when we consider the two ways in which two-dimensional Newtonian mechanics could be embedded into $\mathbb{R}^3$, we thereby offer up two different sets of

---

[91] See, for example, Weatherall (2016), Rosenstock and Weatherall (2016), Nguyen et al. (2020), and references therein.

[92] A motivating example here is Weatherall's (2016) condition of theoretical equivalence categorical equivalence, via an equivalence that preserves empirical content.

empirical consequences (making some natural assumptions about the observational capacities of an observer in $\mathbb{R}^3$). This, then, offers a way of saying more than crude positivism or crude formalism – but without helping oneself to overly rich notions of meaning and interpretation.[93]

This also suggests that philosophers interested in questions of structure and equivalence would do well to attend to the topic of empirical content. Although we have touched on this notion at various points in the above (especially, in Sections 3 and 6), it must be admitted that our treatment was partial and superficial. The challenge, I suspect, will be to articulate an account of empirical content that is sufficiently general and abstract to be broadly applicable across a range of theoretical contexts; and yet which is sufficiently concrete to make contact with the rich literature on data and modelling in actual scientific practice. Doing so will not be easy. However, if the above is correct, then this task will be a necessary precondition for giving an appropriate account of theoretical equivalence, and hence – perhaps – for underwriting the realist project more generally. For, as Sklar (in the same piece as was quoted above) puts it:

> Positivism, for all its defects, offers us a theory of theoretical equivalence neatly integrated with its theory of confirmation and its theory of explanation. The realist is obliged to do the same.[94]

This Element has certainly not met Sklar's challenge. I hope, however, to have provided insight into some of the tools that might help someone else do so – or, at least, encouraged the idea that the challenge is worth working toward.

---

[93] Compare Weatherall (2021), Weatherall (2020).
[94] Sklar (1982), p. 108.

References

Alexander, H. G., editor (1956). *The Leibniz-Clarke Correspondence*. Manchester University Press, Manchester.

Andreas, H. (2017). Theoretical Terms in Science. In Zalta, E. N., editor, *The Stanford Encyclopedia of Philosophy*. Metaphysics Research Lab, Stanford University, fall 2017 edition. https://plato.stanford.edu/archives/fall2017/entriesheoretical-terms-science/.

Andréka, H., Madarász, J. X., and Németi, I. (2007). Logic of Space-Time and Relativity Theory. In Aiello, M., Pratt-Hartmann, I., and van Benthem, J., editors, *Handbook of Spatial Logics*, 607–711. Springer Netherlands, Dordrecht.

Andréka, H., Madarász, J. X., and Németi, I. (n.d.). Defining New Universes in Many-Sorted Logic. https://old.renyi.hu/pub/algebraic-logic/kurzus10/amn-defi.pdf.

Awodey, S. (2010). *Category Theory*. Oxford University Press, Oxford.

Barbour, J. B. (1989). *Absolute or Relative Motion: A Study from a Machian Point of View of the Discovery and the Structure of Dynamical Theories*. Cambridge University Press, Cambridge.

Barrett, T. W. (2015a). On the Structure of Classical Mechanics. *British Journal for the Philosophy of Science*, 66(4):801–828.

Barrett, T. W. (2015b). Spacetime Structure. *Studies in History and Philosophy of Science Part B: Studies in History and Philosophy of Modern Physics*, 51:37–43.

Barrett, T. W. (2020). Structure and Equivalence. *Philosophy of Science*, 87(5):1184–1196.

Barrett, T. W., and Halvorson, H. (2016a). Glymour and Quine on Theoretical Equivalence. *Journal of Philosophical Logic*, 45(5):467–483.

Barrett, T. W., and Halvorson, H. (2016b). Morita Equivalence. *Review of Symbolic Logic*, 9(3):556–582.

Barrett, T. W., and Halvorson, H. (n.d.). Mutual Translatability, Equivalence, and the Structure of Theories.

Brading, K., and Brown, H. R. (2004). Are Gauge Symmetry Transformations Observable? *British Journal for the Philosophy of Science*, 55(4):645–665.

Brading, K., and Castellani, E., editors (2003). *Symmetries in Physics: Philosophical Reflections*. Cambridge University Press, Cambridge.

Brown, H. R. (2005). *Physical Relativity: Space-Time Structure from a Dynamical Perspective*. Oxford University Press, Oxford.

Butterfield, J. (2006). Against *Pointillisme* about Mechanics. *British Journal for the Philosophy of Science*, 57(4):709–753.

Butterfield, J. (2011a). Emergence, Reduction and Supervenience: A Varied Landscape. *Foundations of Physics*, 41(6):920–959.

Butterfield, J. (2011b). Less Is Different: Emergence and Reduction Reconciled. *Foundations of Physics*, 41(6):1065–1135.

Button, T., and Walsh, S. (2018). *Philosophy and Model Theory*. Oxford University Press, Oxford.

Carnap, R. (1958). Beobachtungssprache und Theoretische Sprache. *Dialectica*, 12(3–4):236–248.

Caulton, A., and Butterfield, J. (2012). On Kinds of Indiscernibility in Logic and Metaphysics. *British Journal for the Philosophy of Science*, 63(1):27–84.

Coffey, K. (2014). Theoretical Equivalence as Interpretative Equivalence. *British Journal for the Philosophy of Science*, 65(4):821–844.

Curiel, E. (2014). Classical Mechanics Is Lagrangian; It Is Not Hamiltonian. *British Journal for the Philosophy of Science*, 65(2):269–321.

Curiel, E. (2019). On Geometric Objects, the Non-existence of a Gravitational Stress-Energy Tensor, and the Uniqueness of the Einstein Field Equation. *Studies in History and Philosophy of Science, Part B: Studies in History and Philosophy of Modern Physics*, 66:90–102.

Curiel, E. (n.d.). On the Propriety of Physical Theories as a Basis for Their Semantics. http://philsci-archive.pitt.edu/8702/.

Dasgupta, S. (2016). Symmetry as an Epistemic Notion (Twice Over). *British Journal for the Philosophy of Science*, 67(3):837–878.

de Bouvère, K. (1965). Synonymous Theories. In Addison, J. W., Henkin, L., and Tarski, A., editors, *The Theory of Models: Proceedings of the 1963 International Symposium at Berkeley*, Studies in Logic and the Foundations of Mathematics, 402–406. North-Holland, Amsterdam.

Demopoulos, W., and Friedman, M. (1985). Bertrand Russell's the Analysis of Matter: Its Historical Context and Contemporary Interest. *Philosophy of Science*, 52(4):621–639.

Dewar, N. (2019a). Ramsey Equivalence. *Erkenntnis*, 84(1):77–99.

Dewar, N. (2019b). Supervenience, Reduction, and Translation. *Philosophy of Science*, 86(5):942–954.

Dewar, N., Fletcher, S. C., and Hudetz, L. (2019). Extending List's Levels. In Kuś, M., and Skowron, B., editors, *Category Theory in Physics, Mathematics, and Philosophy*, Springer Proceedings in Physics, 63–81. Springer Nature, Cham.

Earman, J. (1989). *World Enough and Space-Time: Absolute versus Relational Theories of Space and Time*. MIT Press, Cambridge, MA.

French, S. and Ladyman, J. (2010). In Defence of Ontic Structural Realism. In Bokulich, A., and Bokulich, P., editors, *Scientific Structuralism*, 25–42. Springer Netherlands, Dordrecht.

Friedman, M. (1983). *Foundations of Space-Time Theories: Relativistic Physics and Philosophy of Science*. Princeton University Press, Princeton, NJ.

Frigg, R., and Votsis, I. (2011). Everything You Always Wanted to Know about Structural Realism but Were Afraid to Ask. *European Journal for Philosophy of Science*, 1(2):227–276.

Glymour, C. (1977). The Epistemology of Geometry. *Noûs*, 11(3):227–251.

Greaves, H., and Wallace, D. (2014). Empirical Consequences of Symmetries. *British Journal for the Philosophy of Science*, 65(1):59–89.

Halvorson, H. (2019). *The Logic in Philosophy of Science*. Cambridge University Press, Cambridge.

Healey, R. (2009). Perfect Symmetries. *British Journal for the Philosophy of Science*, 60(4):697–720.

Hellman, G. P., and Thompson, F. W. (1975). Physicalism: Ontology, Determination, and Reduction. *Journal of Philosophy*, 72(17):551–564.

Hodges, W. (1993). *Model Theory*. Number 42 in Encyclopedia of Mathematics and Its Applications. Cambridge University Press, Cambridge.

Hudetz, L. (2019). Definable Categorical Equivalence. *Philosophy of Science*, 86(1):47–75.

Ismael, J., and van Fraassen, B. C. (2003). Symmetry as a Guide to Superfluous Theoretical Structure. In Brading, K., and Castellani, E., editors, *Symmetries in Physics: Philosophical Reflections*, 371–392. Cambridge University Press, Cambridge.

Jacobs, C. (forthcoming). Absolute Velocities Are Unmeasurable: Response to Middleton and Murgueitio Ramírez. *Australasian Journal of Philosophy*.

Ketland, J. (2004). Empirical Adequacy and Ramsification. *British Journal for the Philosophy of Science*, 55(2):287–300.

Knox, E. (2014). Newtonian Spacetime Structure in Light of the Equivalence Principle. *British Journal for the Philosophy of Science*, 65(4):863–880.

Kosso, P. (2000). The Empirical Status of Symmetries in Physics. *British Journal for the Philosophy of Science*, 51(1):81–98.

Lévy-Leblond, J.-M. (1971). Galilei Group and Galilean Invariance. In Loebl, E. M., editor, *Group Theory and Its Applications*, 221–299. Academic Press, New York and London.

Lewis, D. (1994). Humean Supervenience Debugged. *Mind*, 103(412): 473–490.

List, C. (2019). Levels: Descriptive, Explanatory, and Ontological. *Noûs*, 53(4):852–883.

Lutz, S. (2012). *Criteria of Empirical Significance: Foundations, Relations, Applications*. PhD thesis, University of Utrecht. http://dspace.library .uu.nl/handle/1874/241030.

Lutz, S. (2015). What Was the Syntax-Semantics Debate in the Philosophy of Science About? *Philosophy and Phenomenological Research*, 95(2), 319–352.

Malament, D. (1977). Causal Theories of Time and the Conventionality of Simultaneity. *Noûs*, 11(3):293–300.

Malament, D. B. (2012). *Topics in the Foundations of General Relativity and Newtonian Gravitation Theory*. University of Chicago Press, Chicago.

Manzano, M. (1996). *Extensions of First Order Logic*. Cambridge University Press, Cambridge.

Maudlin, T. (2018). Ontological Clarity via Canonical Presentation: Electromagnetism and the Aharonov–Bohm Effect. *Entropy*, 20(6):465.

Maxwell, G. (1968). Scientific Methodology and the Causal Theory of Perception. In *Studies in Logic and the Foundations of Mathematics*, vol. 49, pp. 148–177. North-Holland Publishing Co., Amsterdam.

Maxwell, G. (1970). Structural Realism and the Meaning of Theoretical Terms. *Minnesota Studies in the Philosophy of Science*, 4:181–192.

Maxwell, G. (1971). Theories, Perception, and Structural Realism. In Colodny, R. G., editor, *The Nature and Function of Scientific Theories: Essays in Contemporary Science and Philosophy*, 3–34. University of Pittsburgh Press, Pittsburgh.

McLaughlin, B., and Bennett, K. (2018). Supervenience. In Zalta, E. N., editor, *The Stanford Encyclopedia of Philosophy*. Metaphysics Research Lab, Stanford University, spring 2018 edition. https://plato.stanford.edu/archives/ spr2018/entries/supervenience/.

Middleton, B., and Ramírez, S. M. (2021). Measuring Absolute Velocity. *Australasian Journal of Philosophy* 99(4), 806–816.

Møller-Nielsen, T. (2017). Invariance, Interpretation, and Motivation. *Philosophy of Science*, 84(5):1253–1264.

Nagel, E. (1979). *The Structure of Science: Problems in the Logic of Scientific Explanation*. Hackett, Indianapolis.

Newman, M. H. A. (1928). Mr. Russell's "Causal Theory of Perception." *Mind*, 37(146):137–148.

Ney, A., and Albert, D. Z., editors (2013). *The Wave Function: Essays on the Metaphysics of Quantum Mechanics*. Oxford University Press, Oxford.

Nguyen, J., Teh, N. J., and Wells, L. (2020). Why Surplus Structure Is Not Superfluous. *The British Journal for the Philosophy of Science*, 71(2):665–695.

North, J. (2009). The "Structure" of Physics: A Case Study. *Journal of Philosophy*, 106(2):57–88.

Pitts, J. B. (2010). Gauge-Invariant Localization of Infinitely Many Gravitational Energies from All Possible Auxiliary Structures. *General Relativity and Gravitation*, 42(3):601–622.

Pooley, O. (2006). Points, Particles, and Structural Realism. In Rickles, D., French, S., and Saatsi, J., editors, *The Structural Foundations of Quantum Gravity*, 83–120. Oxford University Press, Oxford.

Przełęcki, M. (1969). *The Logic of Empirical Theories*. Routledge and Kegan Paul, London.

Psillos, S. (2000). Carnap, the Ramsey-Sentence and Realistic Empiricism. *Erkenntnis*, 52(2):253–279.

Quine, W. V. (1951). Ontology and Ideology. *Philosophical Studies: An International Journal for Philosophy in the Analytic Tradition*, 2(1):11–15.

Ramsey, F. P. (1931). Theories (1929). In Braithwaite, R. B., editor, *The Foundations of Mathematics and Other Logical Essays*. Routledge and Kegan Paul, London.

Read, J. (forthcoming). Geometric Objects and Perspectivalism. In Read, J., and Teh, N., editors, *The Philosophy and Physics of Noether's Theorems*. Cambridge University Press, Cambridge. http://philsci-archive .pitt.edu/18911/.

Read, J., and Møller-Nielsen, T. (2020). Motivating Dualities. *Synthese*, 197(1):263–291.

Read, J., and Teh, N. J. (2018). The Teleparallel Equivalent of Newton–Cartan Gravity. *Classical and Quantum Gravity*, 35(18):18LT01.

Redhead, M. L. G. (1975). Symmetry in Intertheory Relations. *Synthese*, 32(1-2):77–112.

Roberts, J. T. (2008). A Puzzle about Laws, Symmetries and Measurability. *British Journal for the Philosophy of Science*, 59(2):143–168.

Rosenstock, S., and Weatherall, J. O. (2016). A Categorical Equivalence between Generalized Holonomy Maps on a Connected Manifold and Principal Connections on Bundles over That Manifold. *Journal of Mathematical Physics*, 57(10):102902.

Russell, B. (1927). *The Analysis of Matter*. Kegan Paul, London.

Saunders, S. (2003). Physics and Leibniz's principles. In Brading, K. and Castellani, E., editors, *Symmetries in Physics: Philosophical Reflections*, 289–308. Cambridge University Press, Cambridge.

Saunders, S. (2013). Rethinking Newton's Principia. *Philosophy of Science*, 80(1):22–48.

Shapiro, S. (1991). *Foundations without Foundationalism: A Case for Second-Order Logic*. Oxford University Press, Oxford.

Sider, T. (2010). *Logic for Philosophy*. Oxford University Press, Oxford.

Sklar, L. (1982). Saving the Noumena. *Philosophical Topics*, 13(1):89–110.

Stein, H. (1967). Newtonian Space-Time. *Texas Quarterly*, 10:174–200.

Swanson, N., and Halvorson, H. (n.d.). On North's "The Structure of Physics". http://philsci-archive.pitt.edu/9314/.

Teitel, T. (2021). What theoretical equivalence could not be. *Philosophical Studies*, 178(12), 4119–4149.

van Benthem, J., and Pearce, D. (1984). A Mathematical Characterization of Interpretation between Theories. *Studia Logica*, 43(3):295–303.

van Oosten, J. (2002). Basic Category Theory. https://webspace.science.uu.nl/ooste110/syllabi/catsmoeder.pdf.

Wallace, D. (2019). Who's Afraid of Coordinate Systems? An Essay on Representation of Spacetime Structure. *Studies in History and Philosophy of Science Part B: Studies in History and Philosophy of Modern Physics*, 67:125–136.

Wallace, D. (n.d.-a). Isolated Systems and Their Symmetries, Part I: General Framework and Particle-Mechanics Examples. http://philsci-archive.pitt.edu/16623/.

Wallace, D. (n.d.-b). Observability, Redundancy and Modality for Dynamical Symmetry Transformations. http://philsci-archive.pitt.edu/16622/.

Washington, E. E. (2018). *On the Equivalence of Logical Theories*. Senior thesis, Princeton University, Princeton, NJ.

Weatherall, J. O. (2016). Are Newtonian Gravitation and Geometrized Newtonian Gravitation Theoretically Equivalent? *Erkenntnis*, 81(5):1073–1091.

Weatherall, J. O. (2017). Inertial Motion, Explanation, and the Foundations of Classical Spacetime Theories. In Lehmkuhl, D., Schiemann, G., and Scholz, E., editors, *Towards a Theory of Spaceme Theories*, number 13 in Einstein Studies. Birkhäuser, Basel.

Weatherall, J. O. (2021). Why Not Categorical Equivalence? In Madarász, J. X., and Szekely, G., editors, *Hajnal Andréka and István Németi on Unity of Science*, number 19 in Outstanding Contributions to Logic, 427–451. Springer, Cham.

Weatherall, J. O. (2020). Equivalence and Duality in Electromagnetism. *Philosophy of Science,* 87(5), 1172–1183.

Wheeler, J. T. (2007). Gauging Newton's Law. *Canadian Journal of Physics,* 85(4):307–344.

Wilhelm, I. (2021). Comparing the structures of mathematical objects. *Synthese,* 199(3), 6357–6369.

Winnie, J. A. (1986). Invariants and Objectivity: A Theory with Applications to Relativity and Geometry. In Colodny, R. G., editor, *From Quarks to Quasars, University of Pittsburgh Press, Pittsburgh,* 71–180. University of Pittsburgh Press, Pittsburgh.

Worrall, J. (1989). Structural Realism: The Best of Both Worlds? *Dialectica,* 43(1-2):99–124.

Worrall, J. (2007). Miracles and Models: Why Reports of the Death of Structural Realism May Be Exaggerated. *Royal Institute of Philosophy Supplements,* 61:125–154.

Zahar, E. (2001). *Poincaré's Philosophy: From Conventionalism to Phenomenology.* Open Court, Chicago.

Zahar, E. G. (2004). Ramseyfication and Structural Realism. *Theoria. Revista de Teoría, Historia y Fundamentos de la Ciencia,* 19(1):5–30.

Acknowledgements

I'm grateful to Jim Weatherall and Cambridge University Press for the opportunity to write this text, and for their help, support, and patience throughout the process. For reading and commenting on earlier drafts, I'm very grateful to Thomas Barrett, Frank Cudek, John Dougherty, Laurenz Hudetz, and James Read; and especially, many thanks to the two anonymous referees from the press for their detailed comments on the whole manuscript. Thanks to Jeremy Butterfield and Bryan Roberts for the invitation to discuss an earlier draft at the Cambridge-LSE Bootcamp in Philosophy of Physics, and to all the participants in the Bootcamp for their comments and insights: especial thanks to Andreas Aachen, Jeremy Butterfield, Erik Curiel, Dominik Ehrenfels, Joanna Luc, Tushar Menon, and Ruward Mulder for sending me written comments. Thanks also to the participants in my course on 'Structure and Equivalence' at the Ludwig Maximilian University of Munich in the winter semester 2020/21, and again, special thanks to Max Binkle and Benjamin Zayton for written comments. Finally, thanks to Julia Ford and Malini Soupramanian for their help and patience with preparing the final manuscript.

This project was supported by the German Research Foundation (DFG), through the provision of a Scientific Networks Grant on 'Category Theory in Philosophy of Science'.[95] Thanks to the DFG for their support, and to all those who participated in the network for valuable discussion. For conversation about these, related, and many other topics, thanks to Thomas Barrett, Erik Curiel, Joe Dewhurst, John Dougherty, Josh Eisenthal, Ben Eva, Hans Halvorson, Stephan Hartmann, Laurenz Hudetz, James Read, Katie Robertson, David Wallace, and Jim Weatherall. For general support and a wonderful sense of philosophical community, thanks to everyone at the Munich Center for Mathematical Philosophy. Thanks to Pierre Chatelier for developing and maintaining the LaTeXiT tool (https://www.chachatelier.fr/latexit/), to Daniel Kirsch for the Detexify tool (https://detexify.kirelabs.org), and to Yichuan Shen for his tikzcd-editor (https://tikzcd.yichuanshen.de/).

---

[95] Gefördert durch die Deutsche Forschungsgemeinschaft (DFG) – Projektnummer 392413352.

This Element was written during a very strange and difficult time – but one that was considerably lightened by several people in it. To Rodrigo and Albin: thank you for being excellent office- and house-mates, when those two categories were unexpectedly combined (and for making so much coffee). To my family: thank you for all the love and support, and for the willingness to listen to endless Zoom updates about my progress. And finally, to A: thank you for being there, and for being you.

.

Cambridge Elements ≡

The Philosophy of Physics

James Owen Weatherall
University of California, Irvine

James Owen Weatherall is Professor of Logic and Philosophy of Science at the University of California, Irvine. He is the author, with Cailin O'Connor, of *The Misinformation Age: How False Beliefs Spread* (Yale, 2019), which was selected as a *New York Times* Editors' Choice and Recommended Reading by *Scientific American*. His previous books were *Void: The Strange Physics of Nothing* (Yale, 2016) and the *New York Times* bestseller *The Physics of Wall Street: A Brief History of Predicting the Unpredictable* (Houghton Mifflin Harcourt, 2013). He has published approximately fifty peer-reviewed research articles in journals in leading physics and philosophy of science journals and has delivered over 100 invited academic talks and public lectures.

About the Series
This Cambridge Elements series provides concise and structured introductions to all the central topics in the philosophy of physics. The Elements in the series are written by distinguished senior scholars and bright junior scholars with relevant expertise, producing balanced, comprehensive coverage of multiple perspectives in the philosophy of physics.

Cambridge Elements ^Ξ

The Philosophy of Physics

Printed in the United States
by Baker & Taylor Publisher Services